The
Know
Maintenance
Perennial
Garden

The
Know
Maintenance
Perennial
Garden

ROY DIBLIK

Timber Press

PORTLAND ◆ LONDON

Portions of this book are based on Roy Diblik's *Small Perennial Gardens: The Know Maintenance™ Approach*, published in 2008 by American Nurseryman.

Published in 2014 by Timber Press, Inc.

The Haseltine Building
133 S.W. Second Avenue, Suite 450
Portland, Oregon 97204-3527
timberpress.com

6a Lonsdale Road
London NW6 6RD
timberpress.co.uk

Printed in China
Book design by Laken Wright
Composition and layout by Stewart A. Williams

Library of Congress Cataloging-in-Publication Data
Diblik, Roy.
  The know maintenance perennial garden/Roy Diblik.—1st ed.
    p. cm.
  Includes index.
  ISBN 978-1-60469-334-8 — ISBN 978-1-60469-494-9 1. Perennials. I. Title.
  SB434.D3683 2014
  635.9'32—dc23
                                                        2013020403

A catalog record for this book is also available from the British Library.

This book is for Mom

Contents

Preface

As a young person growing up in Berwyn, Illinois, an older suburb of Chicago, I remember planting kohlrabi seedlings with my grandmother in the sliver of a garden alongside the garage. Each day after hanging some laundry and talking with the neighbor over our privet hedge, she would find her way to that small patch of plants and joyfully tend to them. In early summer my Bohemian grandma and her son, my dad, would sit together at the kitchen table, talking. Their time together was a celebration. He would peel and slice up the season's first kohlrabi, and they both made sure I had a few pieces. That was their shared harvest, their crop, their connection to the past, recalling a time when the family nurtured larger gardens with relatives who had passed away or who were now living very different lives. And for me, this memory from my earliest years together with the life experiences that followed—especially my years as an outdoor education teacher in Chicago and as grounds supervisor for the St. Charles Park District—led me to the Natural Garden Nursery in St. Charles, Illinois.

It was 1978, and I was the nursery's first employee—hired not for my horticultural knowledge but for having a good Bohemian work ethic and the simple love of being outdoors. That September I planted my first perennials, 25 bare-root *Campanula carpatica* divisions; I surrounded each with mushroom compost and watered until both compost and soil was thoroughly wet. Every movement and moment was new to me. I made that first planting without any knowledge of what a campanula was, where it came from, who its native companions might be, and why it was loved. But it got me thinking about how little I knew about plants.

Like most folks, I was aware of our shared life with plants, their physical beauty, and their continuous contributions to our health and well-being as sources of food, shelter, and sheer joy. But I had never considered how beautifully they lived among themselves, in strong, healthy communities that have thrived on their own for millenia, with no human intervention. They share their own language, one that we have either ignored or misread. When it comes to deciding what constitutes the good life, our own needs and self-importance have prompted us to drown out and speak for other living beings.

This book is my opportunity to encourage you—the reader, the homeowner, the ecologist, the environmentalist, the youth, the partner, the elder—to listen to the language of plants, to learn what they are and what they need. Go outside, get away from the world of human-dominated activity, and garden.

TOP Health and beauty flourish together in a close-knit, diverse plant community, whether in a garden or in nature.

BOTTOM LEFT The restful mid-November beauty of a true prairie restoration, the Schullenburg Prairie at the Morton Arboretum, Lisle, Illinois.

BOTTOM RIGHT The gentle, soft brown texture of *Sporobolus heterolepis*, the narrow blue foliage of *Carex flacca*, and the mounded gray-brown of *Calamintha nepeta* together create a similar expression of autumn's prairie beauty.

Introduction

This book is about gardening in a new way—one that is in harmony with how plants grow and interact with each other in nature. All it requires from you, the reader, is that you come to know your plants. Once you acquire that knowledge, you will discover that you actually need to spend far less time maintaining them, because they exist in largely self-sustaining communities. I call this new way of gardening the "Know Maintenance" approach—and it can be applied to everything, not just the garden. Simply consider whether you can care for something before you add it to your daily activities. If you can't, you wait until you're able to.

All the plants featured in the book are perennials; all have a very generous, forgiving nature and can have a good life in many parts of our country (broadly speaking, its northern half). I have used only perennials for two reasons. The first is simple: these are the plants I know and grow well. Secondly, I believe perennials provide a solid beginning, middle, and end for durable, diverse, beautiful gardens. In the next few chapters, as you become familiar with the approach, you will start to recognize how and when you can add annuals, vegetables, herbs, shrubs, trees, and containers to these perennial plant communities.

But before I turn to the various aspects of my perennial garden system, we need to look at traditional gardening practices, the source of so much frustration and so many false starts and unfulfilled promises. They have given gardening an undeserved reputation for being difficult and time-consuming. Think about how these practices have evolved over the years. They were designed for specific kinds of plants and site conditions, everything from agricultural crops to bedding annuals, perennials, groundcovers, shrubs, and trees. The problem is, over the last fifty years these well-defined cultural practices have been homogenized into common tasks that are now applied indiscriminately to all types of plants and landscapes. As a result, what is routinely done in most gardens has become less life-enhancing and more overwhelming to both the plants and the gardener. Doesn't look very good, either.

Here is the default American planting look: wood-chip mulch with plants spaced wistfully apart, eliminating the beauty of intimate plant relationships. America the Beautiful is now just the land of the neat and tidy.

Too many homes in too many neighborhoods look like this. These traditional landscapes of evergreens, deciduous shrubs, and lawn require a lot of maintenance. Is it possible our yards could be more beautiful and the time we spend in them more gratifying?

Here are a few common actions or stances that are detrimental to healthy perennial plantings or that inhibit the plant's full potential:

• Rototilling every new planting space, regardless of site conditions.
• Incorporating large amounts of manure and compost into every new planting space, without regard to plant selections (and preferences) and existing soil conditions.
• Placing plants so far apart, they barely touch each other as they mature.
• Applying 2 to 4 inches of wood-chip mulch annually, without considering the product's source and its effect on perennials.
• Deadheading immediately after bloom simply because that's what's "done."
• Staking, caging, or tying up any perennial that begins to lean.
• Cutting back everything and removing all plant debris at the end of the growing season.
• Watering too often and too much, or too little.
• Using too much fertilizer and pre-emergent herbicides.
• Planting only the newest selections, believing they must be superior.
• Trusting that the newest market products will save time and effort.
• Fearing all insects.
• Following tradition blindly.

As you walk down your block, drive through your neighborhood, travel from city to city and state to state, you will notice most perennials are living in a sea of wood-chip mulch, irrigated at least three times a week for twenty minutes—or not at all. Most of these plantings will have large empty areas. The uninhabited areas were planted originally, but the plants eventually died. What caused so much decline? No one took the time to get to know the plants. The owners may have read about the plants' flower type, color, bloom time, and height but neglected to fully take in how and where the plants lived their lives and their intimate association with other plants. They assumed that every planting can be maintained in the same way: weed, add wood chips, then replace dying plants—often.

Imbalance in the garden develops when we don't understand how individual plants live and flourish and how they relate to other plants. By coming to know our plants, we interact with natural elements. We become aware of our evolving relationships with other living things. We understand the custom nurturing necessary for the plant communities we have developed. In the end, the time we spend gardening becomes manageable, and both we *and* our gardens will develop, in the best sense, each time we enter them.

We must abandon the tradition that one method of gardening fits all plantings. We must be more creative with our thinking, our approach, and our participation. And we need to establish new gardening traditions, modeled after the knowledge, awareness, spirit, and joy we bring to each day. So, what should we do in the garden?

• Stay involved! Be attentive!
• Look to nature, both without and within.
• Keep things simple.
• Dream ahead, and yet recognize the beauty of the present.
• Redefine the rules.
• Look for relationships—that's what holds things together.
• Share and participate.

RIGHT The lawn appears to be forcing the plants against the house. This tension creates more work; a lot of pruning and edging is needed to keep each planting group from infringing on the other.

BOTTOM This collection of hostas appears to wander in a wood-chip wasteland. In so many gardens you see more wood than living plants. That's sad!

LEFT The random placement of plants and spotty use of hardscape doesn't inspire any emotional reaction to our surroundings.

BOTTOM This "no cutting the corner" garden space serves a useful purpose and is a pleasant addition to the site, but it is not exactly knitted to it. The plants live confused with their role and relationship to each other.

The Know Maintenance approach isn't just a set of rules; it's also a philosophy, a way of looking at the world and at ourselves. The following beliefs are at its core; they reflect the wholeness of your garden and your continuous relationship with it:

- Beauty is in everything, everywhere, and always re-created. Sunrises, rainy evenings, grandchildren, dogs, a nice dinner, a walk, family, friends. That's how we live.
- Art is a habit we should never break. Painting the house, taking pictures on our travels, cooking meals, choosing a new sofa—all tap the creative part of us.
- Community awakens us to our place. It's our culture, where and how we live and relate to all our neighbors and friends. It's the wonderful diversity of our lives.
- Ecology is being aware that we coexist, living lovingly with others. It's where we are—the sky, this moment, every leaf you'll ever see—and it's also places we cannot see: distant woods, snowy mountaintops, wide oceans, a village in Italy, a small park in Sweden.
- Health is what keeps each of us living in the present

and looking forward to tomorrow. We all try to make intelligent choices that will keep us well, physically and mentally. That same impulse should bring us into the garden, where we can savor the joy of simply being outside.

Everything we have must be cared for: we brush our teeth, wash our clothes, store our food, vacuum our rugs, change the oil in our cars, reroof our homes. The garden is no different. The Know Maintenance approach is based on a single premise: we must have the capability to maintain what we plant. This requires that we know our plants intimately. But it also requires time, and we all lead busy lives. We need to figure out how much time we can give to the garden, and when during the day, week, or month we can give it. Here's how and why the approach works:

- The suggested 140-square-foot garden plans can be treated as building blocks or modules.
- Only durable, selected plants that can be expected to thrive throughout a wide region of North America are featured.

Here are some questions about gardening, to get you thinking. They may not seem directly related to how you garden, yet; but each one clearly connects you to your plants, the earth, the rain, the sun, beauty, health, and art, and circles back to you.

- When was the last time you walked through a remnant prairie?
- What's your monthly average rainfall from May through September?
- Where does your water come from and where does it go?
- What is organic matter? Where does it come from, and why is it important? Can you have too much of this good thing? (Does a tomato have the same needs as a prairie grass?)
- How do the plants you have chosen move through the earth? At what rate do they travel, and what circumstances affect their rate of movement? Is the development of your plants' root systems compatible with the soils and water available?

- How long does it take any given plant to develop from youth to maturity, both in a single season and through the years?
- When do foxtails germinate? When does chickweed germinate?
- What does ecology mean to you?
- How important is diversity in your life?
- Have you allowed plants some freedom in your garden?
- Do you see beyond the object? What are the morning, afternoon, and evening colors of the sky?
- What's your favorite insect or bird?
- How do you define waste and debris?
- How do you find beauty in the world?

These questions don't need quick answers. As you garden, the answers will develop and more questions will arise, and the answers to those will develop, followed by more questions. You will be asking and answering questions happily, feeling good, expanding your possibilities. You will become a thoughtful gardener, sharing a deeper language of beauty, health, and ecology.

- The key plants are arranged in tested combinations that will enable them to live well collectively with minimal input.
- Once you have lived with and cared for them for a few years, you can make changes—not because you have to, but because you want to.
- As you come to know how each plant lives and grows, you will gain insight into how they might fit into your garden.

As you look at the images of the living gardens in this book, move beyond the colors to "see" the textures and structure of their inhabitants, the close intimacy of the plants, the sense of community. Each plant combination has certain maintenance requirements, and in each garden the plants are contributing to their own health and well-being. It all comes down to relationships and partnerships!

So, start small. Be patient, be understanding, be thoughtful, creative, and caring. Sort out what makes sense for you. It's all a shared, step-by-step exercise. Now, let's get going—140 square feet at a time.

OPPOSITE Plant communities live well in all locations. Site determines the plant palette, care determines the selection of plants, and composition provides the beauty.

TOP In autumn, perennials enhance at eye level all the beauty the deciduous tree canopies have always claimed as their own.

Chapter 1

Understanding Your Garden

The Know Maintenance approach is not a do-nothing system, but it does start in a special place: it takes into account the conditions you have and incorporates plants that have a forgiving nature—of the soil, light, and water conditions, of the climatic conditions, and of you, the gardener. The plants that I and others have come to depend upon, the ones featured in this book, can live modestly in varied garden situations prior to your having complete knowledge of their needs. They'll bear with you while you're on your learning curve.

With the Know Maintenance approach, you will see why using regional leaf compost and cutting back your garden adds to the health of the soil and plants. You will think more about water, its relation to the plants, and its journey through the soil. It goes without saying your active involvement is as necessary as the soil, plants, water, and light. You can't be the outsider. Beauty is in the doing!

Start by introducing yourself to your site—the light, the soil, the lay of the land. A garden's location is the single most important aspect of gardening. Ask some questions. The information you gather will lead you toward intelligent gardening practices and an intimate bond with your garden and its inhabitants.

How much light does your site receive?

Look up! How much sunlight does your site receive? You know the term "full sun." But what does it really mean? On the short side, it's direct light between 10am and 3pm, about five hours. On the long side, it's sunrise to sunset. Easy!

"Light shade" means less direct sunlight. Think of large trees growing a distance from each other; through the day, as the sun moves across the sky, there are moments of direct light, then filtered shadows. Say your house is west-facing, and across the street is a mature deciduous tree. Each day beginning at about 3pm, as the sun moves east to west and drops behind that tree, its branches and foliage will lightly shade your front yard. It's like a partly cloudy day, only much more consistent.

"Part shade" results when trees are closer together, with outer branches just about touching; there are thus fewer moments of direct light and more filtered shadows from branches and foliage. For a south-facing house, as the sun moves east to west, filtered light will come through the foliage from midmorning to late afternoon. As the trees age, more light will be available because of branches dropping. Keep in mind that fast-growing trees like silver maples often have a short life span, so you may find that you're back to full sun sooner than you expected.

"Full shade" means that there is little, if any, direct light, no matter the prospect, as in situations where the branches of large shade trees are closely intermingled. Any light that gets through is very soft and gentle. Extreme deep shade occurs in natural sites like the tree-covered north side of a moderate slope or ravine; direct light is almost entirely absent. Another example would be a four-story north-facing condo, fronted by old street trees. Very little direct light penetrates through the trees, and the building itself casts a dense shadow as the sun moves from east to west. Most likely you have seen these kinds of locations, filled with narrow-leaved *Hosta lancifolia*, the soil covered by patchy growths of moss and lingering vinca or pachysandra. Keep in mind that no plant on earth evolved living in the heavy shade of buildings! To find plants that can thrive in these conditions, we should return to that ravine and its north-side plant communities.

RIGHT In this light shade situation, the earth of a prairie savanna is covered with plants. As you deepen your understanding of light conditions, your relationship to exposed soil will change.

LEFT Light sharpens edges, enlivens colors, gives visual substance to all objects, sneaks through leaves and branches, and moves around our buildings. It awakens everything we see.

As you think about light—its source, availability, and the way it reaches the earth—try to develop an awareness of its intensity and how it changes throughout the day and throughout the seasons. Get acclimatized to your place. All plants live in varied light situations. You are the connection to where your plants are placed. You need to see for them. Your understanding of light—daily and through the season—will determine how well they'll live.

What is your soil situation?

Look down! Soil is key to a successful planting. The more you understand its value and learn to contribute basic components that provide for the early needs of the plants you have selected, the better your garden will be. You will find there is no silver bullet, but you will also understand why some soil amending efforts are—or are not—needed.

Soil is a tremendously complex topic, much deeper than you'll need to understand in order to grow and care for healthy plants. Yet you must have a sense of its energy, its vitality. Soil consists of living and dead organic beings and a variety of rocks weathered into the most diminutive pieces. It's the simple skin of the earth that shares its vibrant life with all other living things—every person, creature, and plant. There's a difference between soil and the material you scrape off your shoes, sweep off the porch, and scrub off your hands, which is affectionately called dirt. Soil is the source of life.

Most of you have poked around and planted something in the earth at some time during your life. Now we need to examine the soil closely, look into some of its general characteristics as they relate to the lives of plants. Feel it, dig into it. Rub it between the palms of your hands, sense its composition. Is it loose and sandy? Or is it dense and heavy, slickly clay-like in texture? It should be open enough to permit good drainage, which allows for oxygen exchange between the roots and the soil. But don't worry if you believe your soil isn't perfect. For now it is enough to simply heighten your awareness: soil is both itself alive

and supports life, providing oxygen, nutrition, and water for plants.

Concerning soil, here's a breathless string of blanket beliefs I'm certain you've heard and possibly practiced. I have! "To prepare your ground for planting, remove your sod, cover the soil with [various inches] of peat moss or sand or well-composted manure, or mushroom compost. Add limestone, milorganite, a blend of fertilizers; spray compost tea on it; use generous amounts of seaweed, rice hulls, packaged fungi and bacteria; then rototill everything in until the soil is extremely friable. Now you are ready to plant." Right? Not necessarily. Plant what? The overarching notion is that anything you plant in this well-fortified earth should have a wonderful life. But that's weak thinking. All plants do not share the same culture and soil requirements. They have lived in various ecological habits from sun to shade and wet to dry; in each case, the soil is aligned with the conditions it finds itself in.

Each component in this buffet of amendments has some purpose in soil development—for various types of plantings. The important thought is this: what soil conditions are necessary to provide a good beginning for the plants expected to grow and live on a specific site? Here's

Not unlike each of us, all plants want to live, given the least "crack" of a chance. They live with purpose, they live with energy, they strive to be healthy, and—if treated optimally—they freely "share the joy" with us.

an example: if you are growing delphiniums, the soil has to be high in organic matter and retain moisture more evenly after a watering, yet not be constantly wet. This soil would need composted manure or mushroom compost worked in. If you start with a dead turf area, dig 2 to 3 inches of your chosen material a foot into the soil, and mulch heavily (taking care not to get the mulch too close to the plant stems, which invites disease), your delphiniums will look fine the first and second season. But it may take a couple more years of amendment for the organic matter and moisture retention to be at a level sufficient to grow truly amazing delphiniums. Be patient. By the third or fourth season, your delphiniums will be breathtaking. Of course, that's if they are also maintained properly.

There are many cases when improving the soil for a specific planting is critically important. The challenge is to know when and why, then amend the specific soil on

You can always look to native plant communities to answer questions about organic matter, spacing, weed control, mulching, watering, light conditions, and intimate beauty. Undisturbed nature has no questions, just patient solutions.

the specific site to fit the needs of the intended planting. We will look at your soil together and examine the plants growing there now and the length of time they have lived there. That knowledge will indicate the condition of your soil and help you to understand what other plants will thrive in your existing soil conditions. The soil will continue to satisfy the needs of present plants, and the new plants will live as they know how.

How do soils accumulate organic matter?

Consider an open field. The dominant grasses could be Hungarian brome grass and orchard grass, two European pasture grasses that grow along most roadsides in the Midwest. The soil here receives organic matter from the constant living and dying of the grasses' roots and from the seasonal dieback of the foliage, which collects on the soil and then decomposes. Look at other areas where plants are growing, and think about how they accumulate

This healthy lawn indicates good soil conditions for a Know Maintenance perennial garden. Many believe the sod should be removed and hauled away and large volumes of organic matter rototilled in. Those beliefs are untrue.

organic matter. Walk over to an empty lot; look at what's growing there, and think about what happens to the yearly accumulation of foliage, stems, flowers, and roots. Where does it all go?

The value of healthy soil is immeasurable, but defining it is difficult. What's healthy will differ, depending on the plants that are selected to live in a certain area. It is common human practice: a person or group of people have a vegetative goal for a chosen site. To accomplish that goal, the soil needs to be sound enough to support the ongoing health of the selected vegetation. The upshot is that if all soils are selected, amended, and managed in the same way, they could prove to be unhealthy for the preferred vegetation—if not right away, possibly later in the planting's life.

Originally, every plant community on earth lived in healthy soil that was sustained by the plants themselves—there was no depletion of resources. Agriculture dramatically changed that. Once we began removing resources from the earth, we needed to learn how to manage the soil so we could continue producing the plants necessary to feed, clothe, and shelter us. The soil became dependent on human input. Its many, many centuries of health

disappeared; its identity, with self-sustaining plant communities, ended. Turf, vegetables, grain crops, soybeans, corn, and horticultural plantings all now require human inputs because we have placed the plants where *we* what them to live, not where *they* want to live.

Why do you think your soil is bad?

Now let's think about the soil in your site. For most of you, the planting area is likely to be the lawn area around your home, whether front or back yard, which is generally very slightly graded to allow heavy rain to run off. The first question is, why do you think your site's soil is bad? If you live in an older home, I am certain you have a moderately healthy lawn. You have taken average to good care of it for a few years, maybe longer. You have good soil! Maybe not good enough to grow competition dahlias, prize-winning pumpkins, or a bent grass putting green, but in ready condition to plant the key perennials featured in this book!

The turf grass has had roots living and dying for years,

At the Shedd Aquarium in Chicago, we killed 8,000 square feet of lawn and covered the area with regional leaf compost. The plant communities were laid out and planted through the compost into the non-rototilled dead sod.

adding organic matter, and the frequent addition of grass clippings has also contributed. My experiences planting in just these conditions indicate you are ready to plant your perennial garden. The plants you will be using in this turf-aged soil are just the ones that can establish well and have a good life after that good start. As it matures, each plant will continue adding organic matter through the living and dying of its roots. You can let the plants live in their own litter, or perhaps you'll decide to mulch with regional leaf compost; either way, it's another contribution to strong, healthy soil.

What about water?

Water is perhaps your most precious resource. Here are some questions to ask and thoughts to have about it, pertaining to your site. When these are answered, you will be in a position to create the best planting approach:

- What's the lay of the land? Observe how your ground slopes—is it relatively flat, or is there a noticeable incline?
- Which way does water flow after a moderate rainfall?
- Do certain areas retain moisture longer?
- Does a particular spot become drier soon and stay dry longer? Why?

Develop an awareness of how water moves into and through the soil, and how quickly or slowly it does so. Many available plants have patiently waited for us to notice that they live well on average rainfall. Think about how much water you'll need to maintain your plantings, and where it will come from.

What if your soil *is* bad?

What if the site you intend for your garden is not the typical planting area? What if it's not that aforementioned, ready-to-plant, flat to slightly sloping front or back area that has been turf for many years? Perhaps you and your family, or if you're single, you, have just moved into a new home. The contractor or developer has just spread a few inches of topsoil around your freshly graded property. Below that topsoil is construction soil, many layers of blended degrees of clay subsoils mixed together. Unfortunately most contractors, developers, bankers, and financial groups don't get too emotional about soil and the life of plants. They do follow weak principles, and some even go beyond, but rarely does soil have value to them. They realize how much time and cost is involved to establish a young turf area.

Now, all those amendments I mentioned earlier? Some of them are important to give you a good start, and that's what you need in this situation: the best start you can afford, involving time and material. I'm going to assume you can't do what many high-end botanic gardens do—that would be, excavate 3 to 4 feet of soil out of your planting area and bring a specially chosen soil in from the floodplain of a local river or have a soil specially blended for your planting goals. Well, you don't need to go to those extremes, and here's why: the selected plants and styles of the Know Maintenance approach have not only a giving, but a very forgiving nature. In chapter 3, "Site Preparation and Planting," we will go through the process of amending this type of soil (yes, rototilling), and in time the plants will flourish and your planting will need less input—but not less awareness—from you.

As I write, it's January in the Chicago area, and we haven't had an inch of snow, last winter very little. Last summer was hot and extremely dry. Our soil moisture is low. Is this an indicator of future conditions for our area?

Future public and residential plantings need to be less dependent on frequently used, non-monitored watering systems. It's time. It's not that we need to make great sacrifices. We just need to manage water as we would manage anything of value and actively promote wise-use concepts. Some cities now collect taxes (or payments, if you prefer) for the volume of runoff from your property that finds its way into the city sewer system after rain events. This money is used to maintain and improve the local system and inspire you to collect and reuse your rainwater.

Possibly you need to consider devising a way to collect rainwater and keep it on your property using rain barrels or cisterns. If you decide to build some sort of rain catchment system, check the recommended reading section; there's an excellent book on rain gardens. Advance at your own pace. Don't try to accomplish too much at once.

Have patience! For most of the giving, forgiving Know Maintenance perennials in this planting, this is June of the third season.

Chapter 2

Understanding Plants

The most intimate experience in the garden is our relationship with plants. We have been involved in this love affair since our ancestors first drew breath. We have no way to separate ourselves from this bond; we can only neglect it, then realize how much that neglect injures us. How should we begin the process of coming to know a plant?

Since we're dealing primarily with perennials in this book, let's begin with a definition. A perennial plant is not a tree or shrub—in other words, it is not woody—and generally lives for three years or more. Are we done? Can we go on? I think we should be a little more determined and have more substance to build on. My favorite definition is from William Cullina's wonderful book, *Understanding Perennials*: "A hardy herbaceous perennial is a plant that survives from year to year in a temperate climate but dies back just above or below the ground at the onset of the dormant season" (Cullina 2009). I like this definition a lot—it's clear, it's relevant to most temperate-zone gardens, and it's easy to understand.

Next, let's look at the various parts of a perennial plant. You're familiar with roots, stems, leaves, and flowers. These are common terms and parts, easily identified. Now it's time to go beyond these general characteristics, to be more observant, looking beyond superficial appearances. This will happen gradually. Start by appreciating that there is much more to observe beyond what you initially see. Hold a leaf, flower, stem, or root in your hand and turn it; look at it from every angle. Then take five or ten minutes to write down what you see and feel, using your own terms and phrases. It's important to constantly observe, relate, and question. As you discover the joy of knowing, note how the distance between you and the plant has lessened.

Let's take a closer look at each part of a perennial, both familiar and perhaps unfamiliar, and look at the ways in which the individual parts of a plant form more complex structures.

Flowers

Almost all of us share the common belief that the beauty of plants consists mainly in their color. It's our most emotional response to gardens. But there's a great deal more to see. As you observe a flower, ask yourself the following questions:

- What shape is the flower, and what are the subtle differences and tones in its color?
- What shape is the bud? What size? Is it the same color as the bloom?
- Do the flowers bloom singly or in clusters?
- How are the individual flowers arranged on the stem?
- Are the flowers scented?
- At what time of day do the flowers open?
- How long does each flower last?
- What pollinators visit the flowers?
- What shape are the seedheads?
- When can you collect seed?

Flowers may occur singly on the stem, or may be arranged in spikes, panicles, or corymbs. Take some time to look these botanical terms up and list three plants for each one.

Foliage

Most gardeners now realize that a plant's foliage is as important as its flowers. Take the time, in the moment and through the seasons, to come to know your plant's leaves. Look at the structure of the foliage, observe the size, and shape. Is each leaf long and narrow? Wide? Oblong? Round? There are many botanical terms describing leaf shapes. Look up these few general ones and list three plants for each: linear, ovate, lanceolate, and spatulate.

Note the color. Is it light or dark green? Does it have a bluish cast? Is it golden? Bronze? Purple? Are the leaves glossy or flat-toned? Do the leaves change colors as they mature from spring into summer? What is the color change

Here in Piet Oudolf's garden, each flower's color highlights its shape and accents the style of the next (yes, even the grasses have flowers).

of leaves as they go from late summer into early winter? When do they drop off? *Do* they drop off? Do the leaves feel rough or smooth? Are they fragrant? What do their edges look like? Here are a few of the many botanical terms used to describe the different edges of leaves. List two plants for each: incised, lobed, serrate, entire, and laciniate.

How are the leaves arranged on the stems? The leaf arrangements on stems use these general botanical terms: opposite, alternate, and whorled. List two plants for each term.

How does the size of the leaf change from early April to mid-May, mid-May to early July? What is the structural change of the leaves from late summer into early winter? As the leaves dry out, do they tend to curl up, hang downward, disfigure slowly until the stems are bare? This characteristic is a quiet change, not often seen as appealing or even thought about at all. But just as with people, the soft, calm outcome of age reflects the season's many beautiful moments.

TOP By mid-May, the developing stems of *Baptisia* 'Purple Smoke' are already sporting flower buds and their signature purple-gray. At every moment of plant development, there is beauty.

BOTTOM LEFT In high season and all seasons, much of the cohesiveness of a planting depends on the interplay of the foliage, both visually and physically.

BOTTOM RIGHT The various stem arrangements, coupled with the equally various shapes and colors of flowers, strengthen the Impressionistic style of this resort garden.

Stems

Stems are the supporting features of the plant, the up-and-down, the slightly arching, the up-and-over, the running-along-the-ground. They hold and display the leaves and flowers; they transport the water and nutrients through the plant. They fit nicely into the vase. They are generally the last of the plant observed through the winter and the herald of the spring's first growth, holding the fresh expanding leaves. Stems are flat, round, square, triangular; smooth or rough, fuzzy or hairy; and of many colors. Now that you have seen all this, look again with affection!

How thin or thick are the stems? Do they grow strongly upward? Are they short and sturdy or long and wiry? What color are the stems as they emerge from the ground, and when does that happen? What color are the stems as they mature through the season? Do the colors change? Do the stems remain strong into and through winter?

Roots

We are not going to become soil scientists just yet, but it is good to be reminded of the exchange that takes place down below, as the roots of your plants collect nutrients and water from the soil. The deeper your awareness of the relationship between roots and the soil, the easier it will be for you to be engaged with the constant, daily renewal of life in your garden.

Are the roots extremely fibrous or thick and fleshy? How thick? How long before they narrow down and become smaller? Do they develop densely or are they looser as they work their way into the soil? How deep do they grow? What color are they? The depth and spreading capabilities of the root system vary with each plant. To develop a sensitivity to this out-of-sight network, investigate and describe, in your own words, the roots of five different plants.

Crowns

The crown is where stems and roots come together. Historically, the term has been used to designate the portion of the plant where new top growth and roots develop each season. In all perennials, the new growth usually takes place here, at or just below the soil level. The crown contains the strength of the perennial; what's more, it can yield a great deal of information about the kind of site and soils the plant naturally prefers, thus providing us

with clues about where the plant is likely to thrive in the garden. This important theme will be restated again and again: provide the plant with conditions similar to those in which it naturally grows.

Let's look at the growth and development of a perennial plant, from the time you purchase it in a container to the point where it's been growing in your garden for three years. In the examples that follow, we'll be paying particular attention to the crown of the plant, and how it develops and expands over that period.

When you buy a containerized perennial, it's in a soilless mix of various components intended for growing a

In spring, all growth comes from the plant's crown, the area supported by roots from which stems and foliage renew themselves. As you can see, this garden has crowns aplenty but is in serious need of some early bulbs!

young plant in a confined space for a short period of time. The plant itself may have started either from seed, from a cutting, from tissue culture, or from a small division of an older plant. These young plants were probably eight to 12 weeks old when they were first placed in the container. Six to 10 weeks later, they are rooted in and ready to go to market. At this point the plant can be removed from the container and planted into the garden, where it will begin to grow, expanding its stems and roots from the crown. What are the dynamics of this process?

Our first example is *Salvia nemorosa* 'Wesuwe'. In the container, many stems grow from the salvia's dense crown. You plant it, and the following spring, after you prune last season's foliage off, you will find small buds, along with small green foliage at the soil surface. The salvia develops its stems and roots from a solid point; as years go by, the new growth will stay in a central area, although it will become slightly looser. If a plant with this particular kind of crown is placed in soil high in organic matter, composted yearly, and watered often, in short order it will need to be lifted and divided to restore its youthful health and performance. By contrast, in lean soil with modest organic matter, living on its own debris or mulched with leaf compost every two to three years and watered only when needed, if at all, the crown will remain tighter and need less dividing or replacing.

Now we will look at *Coreopsis verticillata* 'Grandiflora'. At point of purchase, you'll note the vertical stems spaced randomly, ½ to 2 inches apart, filling the container. The crown is composed of short, yellow rhizomes that grow close together. You plant it, and the following spring, after pruning off last year's foliage, you will notice small rosettes of fine-cut narrow foliage at ground level, spaced similarly to the pattern you saw in the container and at this point not much larger. In three years, however, the crown of the plant will be 10 to 14 inches wide. This indicates an open, spreading, rhizomatous growth habit, but because the rhizomes are short, you probably won't have trouble controlling the plant. And unlike the salvia, with its dense, tight crown, this coreopsis is capable of taking up more space at a faster rate. Again, this provides a clue about how to position the plant in relation to other plants.

These two types of crowns are the main forms of growth associated with the plants discussed in this book. Each perennial will vary slightly, but you won't have trouble getting a sense of the variations. As you garden, continue to observe and recognize the crown of each plant. The more you know, the better everything will go for you and your garden.

TOP LEFT The flowering stems of the *Echinacea pur-purea* and *Sporobolus heter-olepis* show a determined vertical appearance, yet the foliage of the sporobolus is soft and mounding. These characteristics can be mixed on plants or very distinct.

TOP RIGHT The white-flowered, mounding growth habit of *Calamintha nepeta* allows the *Echinacea pur-purea* to mix in. You will begin to see and create rich combinations like these: just come to know the plants.

RIGHT All three growth hab-its blend into one, inspiring a style and crowding out weeds. This planting is in its fourth season.

Growth habits

All living beings develop in their own characteristic way. We grow upward and outward. So do perennial plants, only they grow downward, too. Understanding their growth habits will provide clues about the rate at which each plant grows through the season and over the years as well as about its ultimate size and shape. This knowledge is crucially important for the placement of plants sharing one garden bed. If plants are correctly placed, they can grow into each other in a healthy way, intermingling and sharing space well. Furthermore, by knowing each plant's growth habit, you'll be aware—even before you put it in the ground—of when dividing or thinning it may be necessary in order to maintain the garden's appearance. As your garden develops, you may decide to let some plants overtake others, but the choice will be yours: you are the artist in the garden.

There are three primary growth habits. Be aware, however, that you will witness the full mature habit of each plant only after you have planted and cared for it for three years:

- **Vertical/upright:** the plant grows noticeably taller than wide (e.g., *Echinacea purpurea* 'Rubinglow').
- **Vertical/mounding:** the plant is only slightly taller than wide (e.g., *Coreopsis verticillata* 'Grandiflora').
- **Mounding:** the plant grows wider than it is tall (e.g., *Geranium sanguineum* 'Max Frei').

At first glance this seems pretty cut and dried, but plants develop with an endless range of heights and widths, so expect some blurring of the boundaries and lots of beautiful moments in the dynamics of your garden. There are no absolutes here; often small changes in soil conditions and moisture can cause a slight increase in the spread or height of a plant in a given season. For example, if *Perovskia atriplicifolia* is mulched yearly with mushroom compost, the high organic matter will cause the plant to be taller but lax, creating a wider, looser look. In addition, because the plant's balance has been disrupted, its life will be shorter. This situation is not overly harmful, yet when you understand that too much care might be giving you more to do (as well as resulting in an unhealthy plant), you can see how learning the language of the plant will save you from wondering "why?" and "what happened?" too many times.

Growth rates

All living beings develop at a certain rate, and eventually our development stops. As winter segues into early spring, perennial plants are all emerging. In the Chicago area, *Salvia nemorosa* 'Wesuwe' is about 2 inches high by April 15; by May 20 it's beginning to bloom. Although warmer or cooler temperatures during that period will cause the growth of foliage and bloom time to shift a little, you'll find that it's pretty consistent for this salvia. This roughly four-week time frame is only a portion of the plant's growing season. When you observe a plant for the whole growing season, your sense of its growth rate will develop further.

Getting a clear sense of a plant's growth rate takes time, observation, and patience. It can be helpful to write down your observations. This will make it easier to recall the characteristics you've noted, which in turn will be enhanced by seeing the plant daily.

Growth rate has to do not only with how the plant develops in one year but also how quickly it reaches its mature size. When you know a plant's growth rate over a number of years, you'll be able to combine it with plants that share a similar rate. Thus each plant can grow with and into its neighbor, being sensitive to the other's developing character. This knowledge will also help you avoid plant thugs—you don't want one plant or group of plants inhibiting the growth and development of the maturing garden community.

In five years, plants will have reached their mature height and spread. From this point the plants will continue to age, and change, as we also do. Our posture droops, our skin wrinkles, our hair grays, our muscles relax and get softer. Sadly, or maybe thankfully, we cannot renew ourselves. Plants, however, *can* be rejuvenated. As perennials age beyond their fifth year, some may need to be divided and replanted; some may seed about and maintain a youthful "appearance" within the garden, albeit at a new spot; and some may need to be thinned along the edges from time to time to maintain the look of the planting.

Here is an example of two plants living together and how their growth rate affects their interactions seasonally and through the years. The two plants are *Coreopsis verticillata* 'Grandiflora' and *Echinacea purpurea* 'Virgin'. A higher percentage of the echinacea is planted because it has a vertical/upright growth habit, whereas the coreopsis has a vertical/mounding habit. The crown of the coreopsis will move it through the soil at a faster growth rate than the echinacea. So what do you look for and what do you do?

About three years after planting, the echinaceas closest to the coreopsis will begin to get crowded by the spreading crown of the coreopsis. You have two options. First, if the percentage of echinacea planted was high enough in relation to the coreopsis, the push of the coreopsis may not be unfavorable to the health and beauty of the planting. If a few echinaceas get crowded out, the scale and proportion of the planting may still look fine, even more integrated. This option allows for more fluid dynamics in the garden. And thanks to the echinacea, you will also have more of the color white and heavier texture from its foliage and seedheads.

On the other hand, if the coreopsis appears to be going in a dominant direction and starts pressuring the echinaceas, in mid- to late April as the coreopsis is emerging, you can dig out some of the crown (the tight rhizomes) around the edges of the plant, reducing its size by half. This division, done every three to four years, should give the echinaceas some breathing room. If the coreopsis needs to be tended often, the initial percentage of echinaceas was probably lower, resulting in a higher proportion of golden yellow to white within the group. You can begin to see how combining plants in different percentages can influence your labor as well as the appearance of the garden.

All together now

Collectively, all the parts we considered in this chapter are all one subject: the plant. They have common needs: light, air, water, the soil, and time. Your practical knowledge of these terms and their relationship to each other will connect you, in a satisfying way, to the healthy plant and enable you to create a healthy garden. You will be freed from one of the most obsessive horticultural

The dark stems of *Amsonia tabernaemontana* var. *salicifolia* emerging from the ground, backed by grape hyacinths and enhanced by *Narcissus* 'Lemon Drops'. That's the artist in the garden, that's you!

passions—expecting the plants to conform to your wants, a state of mind that usually results in failure, frustration, and a loss of self-confidence. Knowing the plant returns you to a natural and intuitive relationship with your garden. Moreover, you will be much less tethered to the marketing and promotional fads of the gardening industry.

To make a successful garden, we must know and understand the whole plant, not just a single part. Understandably, we all tend to focus on the beauty of the flower—its color, its shape, and its universal fascination. The flower is most strongly linked to beauty, comfort, peace, healing, love, and prosperity. And without question, flowers are essential to the garden. But the same passion has to be felt for foliage, stems, roots, crowns, and the day-to-day changes these parts experience over time. Of course, you're already involved with your plants—you find them, buy them, plant them, move them, watch them live, and wonder why they die. You probably know if the foliage feels rough, the stems are red, the roots are long and thick. You simply need to nurture that appreciation until it's every bit as intense as your love of flowers. You need to embrace even the less conspicuous parts of the whole plant. Let's look at a couple of examples.

Take *Geranium sanguineum* 'Max Frei' (bloody cranesbill). As well as its obviously wonderful aboveground characteristics, belowground it has a thick, fleshy, pencil-like root system that spreads modestly yet tightly, creating dense foliage. The roots thrive in drier soils but also transition nicely to moister conditions. Its hidden attributes are likely to be overlooked, but once recognized, you'll love this plant even more for the diverse planting opportunities it presents.

A second example: the stems of *Amsonia tabernaemontana* var. *salicifolia* (willow-leaved bluestar) are essential to the beauty of the plant. When they emerge in April to early May, their color is very dark—almost black. As the stems develop vertically through May, they change to medium gray. Think about the artful bulb combinations you could create interacting with the neutral of these dark stems. That's only one possibility; the combinations, just with the seasonal change of foliage and stems, are limitless.

All plants have unique qualities. We tend to define their strengths and weaknesses based on cursory visual perception, but we must dig deeper to combine them successfully into a working whole. The Know Maintenance approach is not just about gardening or planting a few perennials; it's about knowing plants and making connections, not separating one action from another. You want to develop relationships, feel their value, and keep enhancing the possibilities. Nothing truly good or beautiful is ever accomplished in isolation or by rote.

Chapter 3

Site Preparation and Planting

Each time you plant a new space, you apply certain garden practices. Your understanding of the "why" behind the processes will help you observe and—critically—respond on behalf of your plants. No one should garden by rote, simply repeating things without thinking about them or trying to understand them.

The discussion here will focus on the soil and the initial planting conditions in your garden—that is, on the ecology of the site. Only by understanding the nature of the garden site can you learn to provide the placement and care your plants want.

Clean slate

First, we need to debunk a few traditional garden beliefs and practices that have been encouraged by gardening shows and magazines but that are actually better suited to vegetable gardens. There is a difference between planting a tomato and an ornamental grass like *Sporobolus heterolepis*.

When I first started growing perennials in the late 1970s, I was determined to give them the best possible growing conditions. I remember watching *Crockett's Victory Garden*. The host, James Crockett, often demonstrated the techniques he used to build good soil. When he was finished, he could easily plunge his hand into the soil up to his wrist. That was what I wanted—rich, deep, organic soils! So in those early days I spread an inch of mushroom compost on all my beds and tilled it 3 to 5 inches deep prior to planting. Then each spring I would place another 2 inches of mushroom compost around each plant. It felt right, the beds looked fresh and

managed, and I believed the weeds would be suppressed by this material covering the ground.

I was wrong. The beds became unruly, and the plants aged quickly. I had problems with rhizoctonia, a soil disease that killed the crowns of many plants. Most of all, the weed populations soared. Henbit deadnettle and chickweed, which grow and seed extensively in highly organic soils, went out of control. My constant use of mushroom compost promoted healthy, high populations of weeds along with the uncharacteristic development and unnatural decline of the perennial plants.

It's true that we need to replenish the soil; the question is, how rich does it need to be for your plants to thrive? For a human being, it wouldn't be healthy to eat a big slice of Key lime pie three times a day. To live well, we

Yearly application of wood-chip mulch stalls new growth. These perennials will never grow tightly together by mid-June, in time to inhibit the development of weeds.

all need a balanced diet. Plants are not that different. Too rich a diet can harm them; in fact, many perennials do best in lean soils relatively low in organic matter, and what organic matter there is develops in the soil from all the plant parts that fall to the ground each year.

Another widespread but unwise practice is the habit of placing a 2- to 4-inch layer of wood chips around everything—annuals, perennials, shrubs, and trees. There is not a plant on earth that has evolved living in a pile of wood chips. Plants aren't equipped to grow outward surrounded by yearly applications of wood. Perennials may linger for some years, appearing reasonably nice, but eventually they will decline and die. Often their crown rots because the wood chips retain moisture from an irrigation system

A common sight in many plantings: too few plants, too much wood-chip mulch, too much water. A lingering death is followed by uncertainty: how to replant the area? So the decision is made: just put more mulch down. A better answer: raise your expectations, and learn from nature!

set to cycle on four to five times a week, whether needed or not. The result? Plants must be replaced frequently.

For example, *Parthenium integrifolium* prefers moderately dry to slightly moist average soil. If you apply a 2- to 4-inch layer of wood chips around the plant, in four to six years the mulch will start to inhibit the growth of the plant's crown. You'll know there's a problem because the plant will have a yellow-green appearance and few flower stems. It will eventually die.

A third dubious practice is the too-wide spacing of plants. Plants have lived intimately in their natural communities for millenia; it's a mistake to think they are more beautiful and healthier separated from each other by large amounts of wood chips. When I first started growing perennials, I unquestioningly placed them on 18- to 24-inch centers. But I had an eye-opening experience in 1982 when I visited a graveyard prairie with Ray Schulenburg, who at the time was curator at the Morton Arboretum. He was assessing the quality of the site to determine

its value as a remnant prairie. Ray marked off about a square meter and asked me to see how many prairie species I could find in it. I got down to the ground and started counting. How little space existed between the plants! Before it was all over, I had distinguished 16 different species. Never before had I considered the density of plants, coexisting comfortably and healthily together.

Optimum spacing on the site will depend on the plants' growth habit, growth rate, and their ability to grow into and even support each other. You'll develop a sense of this as your understanding grows. Meanwhile, the garden plans and the forgiving nature of the plants featured in this book are there to help *you* grow.

Siting the site

The first step is to identify what areas of your yard are the best candidates for your new perennial planting. Again, healthy, established lawn areas in the front and/or back yards are typical of many American homes—perhaps yours as well—so one possibility would be a turf area along a sidewalk, patio, deck, or island bed. Another good choice would be a shaded area where existing turf is nice but patchy, due to the lack of light. Another is anywhere vegetation is growing well but has outlived its usefulness. Everything has its moment! It's a given, of course: whatever site you choose, your choice of plants will need to be appropriate to its available level of light and moisture.

In any case, the existing soil is growing plants nicely based on the overall conditions. But how can you be sure that it will also support a healthy group of selected perennials? Your main clue is that the site's existing plants are living well. For years, their roots have been living and dying, thus continuously adding organic matter to the soil and enhancing all the living elements to build a system of moderate health.

Now let's look at one more site, the grounds of a new home, just completed. All the contractors are leaving, the lawn is greening up, the developer graciously planted a few small saplings—other than that, it's a home ready to share and create wonderful memories and an empty outdoor space waiting to be beautiful. But the construction process has left a very unnatured earth. Here's what's happened so far:

1. The topsoil was removed, piled up, and stored.
2. The foundation was dug out, and the subsoil was piled up and moved around the construction site, so as not to interfere with the builders.

3. As the home was being completed, a few holes were dug to bury much of the garbage, to save costs on Dumpsters.
4. The site is regraded, the subsoil moved to its final spot, to promote water movement away from the home.
5. The developer courteously replaces 2 to 5 inches of topsoil around the home, following the earlier grading patterns.
6. Irrigation systems are installed, and the timers are set by the irrigation contractor to water based on generic turf requirements.
7. Sod is laid from the home outward to a certain distance, leaving the remainder of the grounds seeded with grass. On other occasions, the entire area is seeded in grass.
8. A few trees are planted and mulched heavily with shredded bark.
9. And if you're lucky, a few large boulders are placed by the driveway and somewhere around the home.

And that's it! Welcome to the creative method that provides upside-down compacted subsoil, covered by a shallow amount of disturbed topsoil.

How are plants supposed to have a chance? The whole process is implemented without the knowledge of what they require to have a good life. The developers, designers, engineers, and contractors have offered us turf and dying trees and shrubs—generation after generation of landscapes whose beauty has evolved to a simpleminded "neat and tidy." And most people living with this believe that's all it can be.

The developer, engineer, and contractor share the same goals: get turf established and place and plant the required percentage of trees and shrubs stipulated by the county, city, or village where the construction is taking place. They have no accountability for results of the plantings after a year. It's up to the new owner. Let's look at how we can develop that area, using soil amendments, in such a way that newly planted plants can at least establish in the unnatured earth. As the plants mature, they'll begin to create a healthy spot for themselves and the soil. It will happen!

So now. Whatever your circumstances—whether you begin with a vegetated site or a new construction site—define your intended space. Use an extension cord or garden hose to lay out your bed. Make sure you're comfortable with its size and shape. It's best to start small, perhaps with one 10- by 14-foot grid (not coincidentally the size of each garden plan in this book). Pace yourself—you can always add to it later, once you've gotten a feel for the planting style and the care it will require. Next, dig in a crisp edge around the space; this will outline your space cleanly and keep any glyphosate (if you decide to use it; see the next section) from bleeding into adjacent areas.

Now the process takes one of two directions: one is the vegetated site, the other is the new construction site.

The vegetated site

Clearing unwanted vegetation is Job 1. If you've chosen a lawn area for your planting, take a close look at what other plants are growing among the turf grass. If you have very small amounts of white clover and dandelion, place layers of cardboard and newspaper covered with leaf compost (you can find details of this approach on the Internet) or black plastic on top of the vegetation so that high temperatures and a lack of light kill the plants. (The plastic is then removed before planting.) Be patient and persistent, and make sure the weeds are dead, along with the grass itself, before planting your perennials.

I have watched folks try to smother out Canada thistle, field bindweed, and quackgrass and have not yet found anyone to be successful. The roots and rhizomes of this vicious trio can rest dormant in the earth and regrow intensely through the layered material. Again, the Internet is a gift of information; you may be able to find a tactic that goes after these three weeds in a determined way. They are persistent competitors to a young planting; not the smallest portion of them can be allowed to remain.

Probably the most efficient way to clear unwanted vegetation is to use glyphosate. I have no desire to promote the unnecessary use of chemicals; my goal when gardening, always, is to keep the use of chemicals to a minimum, and when I do use them I have sound reasons and support them with a solid outcome. If you decide to use glyphosate, mix it carefully according to directions and spray the intended site. Be careful not to step in it as you're spraying—otherwise, when you walk away you'll leave dead footprints on your turf. Wait 10 to 14 days; see what you missed, and spray the area one more time. Remember: everything has to be dead. This may sound cruel, but you are on your way to developing durable plantings that will grow, live, and provide health for your soil, your plants, and yourself for years and years. Now you are done using glyphosate for the life of the garden—it's a one-time use. The only other chemical you'll ever have to add is H_2O.

Do not rototill or spade the soil. Rototilling disturbs the soil's structure and brings a large volume of weed seeds to the surface, which will then have an opportunity to germinate and overwhelm the young planting. The dead turf and vegetation provide good organic matter, and the undisturbed soil will have few weed issues during the

Here we have killed the sod with glyphosate and are getting ready to lay the plant communities out and plant through the dead sod: it's fine, free organic matter. By not rototilling, we are discouraging heavy, quick weed competition.

nurturing stage of development. The few weeds that do come up will appear mostly around the perennials, and they can be easily removed with a Dutch push hoe. The result of this process is less labor and healthier plants. A good beginning!

Water the area deeply; this will make it easier to dig into and plant. Cover the area with 2 inches of leaf compost; this will be your only soil amendment. Water the plants in the containers well, too, and lay them out, using the templates in chapter 6.

The new home construction site

After your planting site is defined, place about 3 inches of organic matter on top of the soil. You could use mushroom compost, leaf compost, composted bark fines, well-composted manure, mixed composts of leaves and wood chips—many composted organic products would be fine. You really don't need to spend money on peat moss; it's a frequent ingredient in container mixes, useful for its moisture-holding capacity and stability, but it's just too costly for large spaces. Don't mix sand in your soil; you will not use the correct percentage, and your soil will turn to concrete.

Now's the time to rototill. Use a good commercial rototiller and begin mixing the organic material into the soil. The machine should reach 8 to 10 inches in depth. If you want to increase your physical activity, you could add an additional inch of organic matter to the 3 inches: prior to tilling, grab your garden spade and dig the compost into the soil, just flipping it over once, but you need to do it deeply (about the length of the shovel head). After you have turned the compost in with the spade, rototill. Now you have the compost mixed into the construction soil.

As I write, I have been told about killing established turf using Borax. I've never tried it but will this year, and I'll talk to others to find out what their experiences have been. We always need to keep learning, and we have to keep trying. The best results come from taking your time and approaching any process intelligently. If you hurry, the only result will be failure. A garden's success can be measured in part by the quiet satisfaction you receive from enjoying your deliberate, careful work in it.

BOTTOM RIGHT After the plants are placed on the dead sod, planting is done through the sod using a drill or a tile spade. (On this job, we mulched with leaf compost after planting.)

TOP Watering the plants in the containers before planting is critical. If you plant them dry, the soil mix in the containers is difficult to rewet, and many of the plants will be under stress right from the beginning. Soak them good!

BOTTOM LEFT The tile spade. This wonderful shovel's narrow design and length is perfect for planting perennials from container or replanting plant divisions. Keep the edge sharp, and the shovel clean. And don't lend it out!

You should not put too much compost on the soil; if it is not mixed proportionately with the soil, you may be planting only in compost and the plants will dry out quickly and not establish well. Also, if a plant is alive going into winter, know that compost will get much colder than the soil, and the crown of the plant will freeze and weaken going into spring; the plant will decline and be smaller than the previous year. Organic matter is an important component, not a magic wand. Like any additive, it serves a purpose only when used knowledgeably: how often, how much, what kind, why, and, above all, when (or when not) to use it.

Now you can follow the same finishing touches as in the vegetative preparation process: water the area deeply, cover the prepared soil with 2 inches of leaf compost, water the plants in the containers well, too, and lay out the plant patterns.

Planting

Planting is a wonderful part of gardening. It's the time to get your hands dirty, the time when the relationship with your garden begins. Once your space is prepared and you've gathered the plants for the selected grid, you're ready to plant. Here are a few guidelines.

- Make sure the container plants are completely watered right before planting.
- Remove the plant from the container, then gently break up the lower roots. This will promote new, rapid root development in all directions.
- Make sure each hole is sufficiently large, and place the plant so it's neither deeper nor higher than the existing ground level.
- As you fill in around the plant, make certain to push the soil firmly back into place. If the soil is too loose, there will be too much air space, and when the plant is watered, the water will rush by the plant. Firm the soil.

The best tool for planting is a tile spade, which you can find at just about any hardware store. A tile spade is a wonderful gardening shovel—it's narrow and strong and digs the perfect hole for a 4½- or 6-inch container. When you start planting, a bit of leaf compost will mix in with the soil, providing a first-year mulch that will help maintain a moderate, even level of soil moisture during the establishment watering program.

If the area you're planting is large, you can also use a two-cycle engine, one-person drill with a 3½- to 5-inch drill bit. Holes can easily be drilled next to each container placed in the new garden, and the plant can quickly be planted and backfilled easily with the loose soil.

Watering

Each plant you place in the garden now depends on you for nurturing and its ongoing health. First up: you need to water them. This first watering is the most critical one for the establishment of the planting. Here's why.

This first-year planting was laid out in early June, with perennials that love the heat of summer. If watering is managed well during the nurturing period, they'll begin to root in quickly. Affectionate care the first two years favors one outcome: a healthy garden.

For at least six weeks and perhaps for as long as a year and a half, the plants have been living in a soil mix that is completely different from the soil in the planting bed, although both provide balanced amounts of air, water, and nutrients for the plants to live well. Even though the plants are now in the ground, they will be drawing moisture from the container mix until the new roots extend into the earth, which can take four to eight weeks. The first watering must therefore saturate the soil mix around the plants' roots and the surrounding earth. You should put at least 1 inch of water down; if your soil was dry, 2 inches or slightly more. The rule is: water deeply. After the first thorough watering, you can wait four to six days before you water again, always deeply.

Now, if you are planting in new construction soil, the soil may hold more moisture for a longer period of time. Let the soil dry out a day or two longer (than the usual four to six, for vegetative sites) after the first deep watering.

In either case, you will have to be the good monitor. The sense of touch and sight will be your greatest guide. Check the soil, and water when it feels drier; look at the foliage of your plants, and know that wilting can also happen from too much water due to the roots declining. Each time you water, let your sprinklers, hose, or irrigation system run to equal 1 inch of rain. Use a rain gauge to measure the amount of water and the length of time it takes to get that 1 inch of water.

Thereafter, water every four to seven days (eight to 11 days in new construction soils), working with the weather, paying attention to rainfall, drying winds, and the daytime temperature. Don't be fooled by cloudy, misty mornings— you may still need to water. Use your rain gauge and a soil probe, otherwise known as your finger. That's right—just stick the length of your finger in the soil around some of the plants and take note of the moisture content. You're the best sensor on the market. There's no computer program that can intimately relate the plants, the soil, and the weather better than you can. Trust yourself, your judgment, and your growth as a thoughtful gardener.

Observe the plants: how do they look? They should be a healthy green. In about five to seven weeks you should start seeing new foliage develop. At this point you can begin to reduce the watering. Always check the weather conditions; if there's plenty of rain, you may need to water only every two to three weeks. This is particularly true as fall approaches—at that time of year, cooler weather and rain showers should keep the soil evenly moist.

As the plants become established, you will develop an understanding of time and its relationship to plant growth, along with a deeper appreciation of the relationship between water and young plants during their transition from container plant to garden plant. These experiences will be yours always.

Weeding the new planting

If you followed the steps outlined earlier to prepare the vegetative site, your perennial bed will have an advantage over all traditional new plantings: the soil has not been rototilled. Not disturbing the soil limits the opportunity for weed seeds to germinate. You will thus have a cleaner planting through the first season. Most weeds that do

The Dutch push hoe is the most important tool you can have. Notice the posture of this "artist in the garden": she's standing upright, no bending! It has a long handle with a nice T grip on one end, so it doesn't dig into the palm of your hand. The agony of pulling a hoe now becomes time well spent improving your posture.

appear will germinate around the plants. In the new construction soil, however, the weed seeds will have prime conditions to germinate and establish, due to the disturbance of the relocated topsoil and the mixed-up subsoil keeping moisture levels slightly higher.

In either case, the best way to deal with weeds is to clean around the plants every two weeks or so with a Dutch push hoe. As the season progresses, weeding may be necessary only every three weeks. Keep the area as clean as possible—and a close lookout for the three thugs: Canada thistle, field bindweed, and quackgrass.

Do not be overly upset with weeds; they are plants with responsibilities. In the next chapter, I have some thoughts to share about these little-regarded plants, which you should also come to know. The better you understand them, the easier they are to control and manage in your garden. The idea is, you can outmaneuver them and respect them at the same time.

Chapter 4

Care and Maintenance

How well we care for something is a reflection of our own well-being. We try to be healthy, and as gardeners we try to keep our plants flourishing, too. Each and every plant in your garden has certain needs to enjoy a good life. Getting to know a plant's needs at the individual level enhances your knowledge of the entire plant community. In the Know Maintenance approach, knowing determines doing. When you care for your plantings actively and intelligently, everything will be more healthy: the soil, the plants, and you. And as your relationship with your planting matures through time, two things will happen. The first will be that now you understand when and how to refine your garden based on the nature of the plants and the style of the planting. The second is that the hard work often associated with gardening diminishes; your activities are more thoughtful, your investment in time is more productive, and increasingly you are relieved by nature's own participation in the gardening process.

This chapter focuses on the care and maintenance of plants within a community. There are two components to this: nurturing and establishment. Nurturing begins immediately after planting, at whatever point in the season that takes place, and continues for two years. Your main concerns during this period will be water and competition from weeds; and, of course, it also involves paying close attention to the plants and their living conditions.

The intimacy of care during the nurturing stage was discussed in the previous chapter. In its simplest form, it's just being a good parent.

Establishment begins the third year after planting. At this time the plants are re

Providing the right level of organic matter

Your goal, remember, is to let the plants live in and with their own decaying leaves and stems, never again removing them from the garden. At planting time you added 2 inches of leaf compost to the surface of the soil. When the perennials reach their second season, you will begin to let them provide their own organic matter. Since the planting is new, there won't be much dead foliage from the previous season; however, in the next three to five seasons, the foliage volume will increase as the plants continue to mature. Here are a couple of ways to cut back your perennials so that the debris will settle back into the garden. The time to do this is early spring (usually March to early April), when the snow is melting and temperatures are warming.

The first is to use your lawn mower, equipped with mulching blades. Set the cutting level on high, and mow all your plants down. Winter conditions will have advanced the decomposition process, making the plants' structure less rigid and much easier to break up. The first time you go over the garden with the mower it will look terrible. Don't worry—go over the area five to seven times. When you're finished mowing, everything should be in small fragments. Now get out your pruners and cut off any stems that may be sticking out at odd angles. The garden should look good to you. If it's difficult to get your mower into the planting area, cut all your plants down the traditional way and rake the debris into a row at the edge of the bed. Then use your mulching mower to chop up the debris and rake it back into the planting bed.

This process brings up an excellent first question. Does this practice work for all perennial plantings? No! Here's why. If the garden is a monoculture planting or a portion of the garden has a high percentage of heavy structural plants, like many of the large ornamental grasses, there will be too much heavy debris to push or ride a mower over. The first lesson, then? The perennial planting needs to be designed with plants of diverse structure. Do not use a high percentage of heavy structural plants like miscanthus, whose stems are too thick and dense to mow. These would need to be cut back with a weed trimmer using a saw blade, cut into smaller sections, then mowed with the mulching mower.

You will learn, through experience, which plants are difficult to mow. And of course, the size of the mower is another factor. A riding mower has more power and is best for large, more open areas. You can maneuver it into smaller areas, just be careful and patient. This practice will feel odd; people watching you will be concerned that you are a confused individual. Take it as an opportunity to share what you now know. And don't have any assumptions about how fast the process should go; when you're finished, the garden will not look like it has in the past. Instinctively, you'll want to start raking everything up. Control yourself: just tidy up what looks out of place—a few dangling stems, some leaves that were missed. Now wait for the bulbs. These are all situations and conditions that will become a normal practice for this style of planting. When you let your plants fertilize themselves, you will have interesting conversations with people and more time to do other gardening activities.

Another method is one I have used in our gardens at Northwind Perennial Farm. We simply cut everything back and lay the debris around the plants. The litter is in much bigger pieces than if it were mowed, so we cut some of the stems into smaller pieces, so that they'll fit comfortably around the plants. I must admit, the first time I did this it was difficult not to run for the rake. "Unwoodifaction"—resisting the urge to mulch with wood chips—is a real test of your resolve. So here's a trick I use: I plant large drifts of early bulbs—mainly chionodoxas and *Narcissus* 'February Gold'. They both come up beautifully not long after the garden has been cut back. Appearing through the layered litter, intermingled with the newly developing foliage of the perennials, the whole site now looks like a beautiful alpine meadow. The airy brown litter quietly sets off the fresh green perennial foliage and the brightness of the bulbs. This practice promotes the beauty of plants over the conventional neatness of mulch, and at the same time encourages the development of a healthy living system.

If the idea of abandoning the use of wood-chip mulch is difficult, I understand. Many of our garden clients are not

When plants knit together and block light, weed seeds have a difficult time developing. The closed plant community then shares in its own care and maintenance. And you are the Impressionistic artist in the garden, creating the patterns and styles. That's much nicer than just being the laborer in the garden.

ready to lose the appearance of fresh mulch, and in some of our gardens we continue to mulch yearly. Here's what we've changed to—and you should, too: just cut everything back and discard it as you normally would. Then, instead of mulching with wood chips, mulch lightly with 1 inch of regional leaf compost. This will provide the fresh spring mulch look many folks have fallen in love with and will not inhibit the ongoing development of your perennials. Plus, you're using a wonderful regional resource. Many villages and cities are now composting their leaves, and bright entrepreneurs are collecting leaves from the municipalities, composting the material, and selling it to homeowners and the landscape industry. You should have an easy time locating this product and supporting the local businesses that are producing it.

Suppressing weeds

Most of us are probably more familiar with weeds than with the plants we'd like to grow. Everywhere we travel, we see many of the same weeds that live in our gardens: in empty lots, along highways, in parks, even in cracks in the pavement. You have to admire their persistence, durability, and ability to live in situations that most of us would consider hostile to plant life. I have a great affection for them.

We need to know more about these plants. Where do they come from? Do they actually fit into natural communities somewhere on earth? How have they managed to survive the constant attention of human beings bent on eradicating them, engaging them with chemicals, hand hoes, enormous cultivation equipment, and endless piles of shredded or chipped wood? And yet they are still with us. These plants were and still are important, even beneficial members of stable plant communities. So what happened? How and why did they come to be perceived as pests?

It was us, human beings. We did one major thing thousands of years ago and continue this activity today. It's called agriculture, and it has destroyed millions upon millions of acres of healthy plant communities, which have been replaced by highly managed commercial crops. The need was there, the need *is* there—we all have to eat. But the fact remains that we have dramatically scarred the earth.

LEFT This 3,200-square-foot perennial garden is being cut back using a mower with mulching blades. Traditionally, this would have taken 33 to 35 hours. For those who Know Maintenance, it takes 45 minutes. It's a great day for the perennials: they are now living like their ancestors, growing healthily in their own debris.

RIGHT Early bulbs transform the look of material that traditionally would have been raked out and hauled away. Here, the litter becomes a beautiful backdrop to *Chionodoxa forbesii*.

Living within all healthy plant communities are certain plants that establish rapidly from seed. If there is a soil disturbance in the community, their seeds will germinate quickly, and the plant will develop and mature at a fast rate, covering the small wounded area and eventually giving way to other more stable plants within the community. With the advent of agriculture, these healing plants had a lot to do. Because of their ability to seed and establish so rapidly, they immediately accompanied the active cultivation of the earth. They lived full lives, in poor lean soils and rich organic soils, building up large seed banks. But because they competed with agricultural crops, they earned the dislike of humans. They became weeds.

The story of weeds is more complex, romantic, and illuminating than I have sketched here. But it's helpful for us all to understand these plants. They are not evil; they have simply responded to the ways in which we have disturbed the earth. In the future, some of these plants may provide us with the ability to green up our cities, or even become sources of food.

In the garden, it is important to come to know these plants. When you understand how they live, and what conditions promote or thwart their growth, you will have an advantage in controlling them. They will not be hated weeds, merely persistent plants that you have outsmarted.

But you need to accept the fact that they will always be present to some degree. If you maintain a healthy plant community and are consistent with your gardening methods, your time weeding will be enjoyable—a good part of being in the garden.

No mercy!

Take the time to know three perennial weeds in particular. They will not be forgiving to you and your planting. Without exception, they have to be eliminated before you install any garden planting.

- All three will be persistent,
  creating hours upon hours of unrewarding work.
- All three create an unhealthy situation for your perennial planting.
- All three detract from the beauty of your plant communities.
- All three have rhizomes that reproduce from the smallest piece left behind.

Don't hope. Put the extra effort into knowing you have done your best to remove these three "Most Unwanteds."

Canada thistle (*Cirsium arvense*)

FLOWER Rosy purple, ¾-inch-wide hairy tufts, branching at the top of the plant.
FOLIAGE 2 to 6 inches, oblong, wavy, crinkled surface with sharp, pointed lobes.
HEIGHT 24 to 48 inches in bloom.
BLOOM TIME Mid-June into September.
GROWING CONDITIONS Average, fertile, well-drained soil in full sun and light shade.
NATIVE LOCATION Eurasia.

In a new planting, remove the thistle and spray with glyphosate; it may take three or four applications. Your first treatment will let the thistle know you are there. Because of the plants' extensive rhizomes, some of them will not respond to the first treatment, and they will stage a comeback. When the new growth is 4 to 5 inches tall, spray the plant again, then again. In established gardens, keep removing the rhizomes, and don't let the plant flower or set seed. The highly viable seed is carried by summer breezes to all parts of your property, germinating quickly, giving you more to do! The easy solution stay with it. You can keep this problematic plant out!

Quackgrass (*Elymus repens*)

FLOWER Narrow, green spikes, 4 to 7 inches long, vertical.
FOLIAGE Flat, ¼ to ½ inch wide, medium green, collectively arching over.
HEIGHT 14 to 36 inches in bloom.
BLOOM TIME June into July.
GROWING CONDITIONS Average, fertile, well-drained soil, full sun to light shade. It begins active growth in the cool temperatures of late March, continuing into June.
NATIVE LOCATION Mediterranean area.

In a new planting, eliminate this perennial cool season grass with a spray application of glyphosate. You may need two applications. Do not begin planting your new garden until you are satisfied the quackgrass is not present its aggressive

rhizomes will penetrate rapidly, growing through and into all your perennials. In established gardens, it's all about persistence. Keep removing as many of the rhizomes as consistently as you can. You may have to dig out some of the perennials, clean the soil off their roots, and pull out the white rhizomes of the quackgrass. Your best control is to keep it out of your life!

Field bindweed
(*Convolvulus arvensis*)

FLOWER Funnel-shaped, white to pink, 1½ inches in diameter. Each lasts one day; seeds are viable in 10 days.
FOLIAGE Triangular to oblong.
HEIGHT The stems can grow up to 18 feet in length.
BLOOM TIME April through October.
GROWING CONDITIONS Average, fertile, well-drained soil in full sun to part shade.
NATIVE LOCATION Europe.

With its twining nature, this spreading vine can consume any garden planting, covering and weaving its way through your plants. The deep, creeping rhizomes continue to develop new plants once the stems are removed. Many times field bindweed is introduced into gardens in the root ball of field-grown trees or shrubs. When you plant these infected new trees or shrubs into your garden, your troubles begin. If you leave a small piece of the root system, it will gain strength and dominate your entire planting. Remember, it's all about the roots!

Other weeds you should know

Chickweed (*Stellaria media*)

FLOWER White, ½ inch, daisy-like, in small clusters at the top of the stem, the

loose stems covering the entire plant.
FOLIAGE Oval, ½ inch long, glossy, growing closely to the stem.
HEIGHT 2 to 8 inches.
BLOOM TIME Mid-April into late May.
GROWING CONDITIONS Average, fertile, well-drained soil in full sun to part shade.
NATIVE LOCATION Eurasia.

The seeds of this winter annual germinate in fall and develop into small, weakly tufted mounds that live through the winter; in late March and early April, they put on strong vegetative growth and flower quickly, seeding around in June and July. A single plant can produce 2,500 to 10,000 seeds. One condition that contributes to the success and spread of this plant are soils high in organic matter—very common in traditional ornamental gardens. Reduce the organic matter content of your soil, and watch the percentage of chickweed decline. Thoroughly remove the developing chickweed in autumn, and get out there quickly in April with your Dutch push hoe to rid the garden of the awakening chickweed. In established gardens, the closed community of your perennials will inhibit the seeds from germinating in autumn by limiting the light that reaches them.

Dandelion (*Taraxacum officinale*)

FLOWER Flat, 1½ inches round, bright yellow.
FOLIAGE Toothed, arrow-like, 4 to 6 inches long, developing close to the ground.
HEIGHT 6 to 18 inches.
BLOOM TIME Early April into mid-May.
GROWING CONDITIONS Average, fertile, well-drained soil in part shade to full sun.
NATIVE LOCATION Europe.

This perennial has a very durable taproot and loves to come back. Each plant can produce 5,000 seeds before the flowering season is over. In the garden, when you do your Dutch push hoeing in late

April into mid-June, you can wear dandelions out by cutting them off below the soil; then by late June, the dense plantings of perennials will prevent them from regaining much strength. You have to be as persistent as the plant!

Henbit deadnettle
(Lamium amplexicaule)

FLOWER Very small, purple, ⅜ inch long, tubular, in whorled clusters.
FOLIAGE Rounded, ¼ inch, round-toothed edges, develops densely on the stems.
HEIGHT 4 to 12 inches.
BLOOM TIME Mid-April into early June.
GROWING CONDITIONS Average, fertile, well-drained soil in full sun to part shade.
NATIVE LOCATION Eastern Europe and western Asia.

This is a quick-growing plant in the cool temperatures of spring, covering the ground and your newly emerging perennials. This weed thrives in highly organic soils; keep the soil lean. In early April henbit deadnettle gives in easily; use your Dutch push hoe and get after it. You'll quickly be relieved of its spreading tendencies. Seeds germinate in autumn and establish extensively before winter; a dense, closed community of perennials inhibits their germination.

Green foxtail *(Setaria viridis)*

FLOWER Spiked, purplish green, 1½ to 4 inches long.
FOLIAGE ⅜ inch wide, 12 to 18 inches long, vertical, slightly arching.
HEIGHT 18 to 36 inches.
BLOOM TIME Mid-July into September.
GROWING CONDITIONS Average, fertile, well-drained soil in full sun to light shade.
NATIVE LOCATION Europe.

The seeds of this annual grass germinate on the warming soils of mid-May and keep it up through the growing season. In new plantings with traditional soil disturbance, they germinate heavily. In late June the closed community of perennials limits their continued germination. Plant into untilled soil to limit foxtails; the foxtails will then germinate more around the planted plant than in the undisturbed soil. This weed is easy to control by Dutch push hoeing in May and June in the open soil between your plants. Begin "observational weeding" in July and August look for the big ones, and if you can get to them easily, out they go.

Annual sow thistle
(Sonchus asper)

FLOWER Numerous, 1½ inches round, flat, bright yellow.
FOLIAGE 2 to 10 inches long, larger at the base of the plant, lance-shaped, lobed with spiny margins.
HEIGHT 36 to 50 inches.
BLOOM TIME July into September.
GROWING CONDITIONS Average, fertile, well-drained soil in full sun to part shade.
NATIVE LOCATION Southern Europe and North Africa.

Reseeds easily, each plant producing about 26,000 seeds annually. It appears visually intimidating, having many spines along the foliage, but when the plant is young, it's easy to pull; the spines are very soft. As the plant ages, the spines can be a little firmer, but you should never experience this: you were Dutch-push-hoeing into mid-June, by which time the perennials will have developed into a closed community, limiting seed germination. In late June through summer, "observational weeding" will eliminate any sow thistles the earlier hoeing missed. The seeds do travel in the air, and they will continue to settle into your garden. Just keep the plant from reseeding on your ground. You can wear this plant out before it does you!

Shepherd's purse
(Capsella bursa-pastoris)

FLOWER ¼ inch long, twice as wide, four-petaled, white, clustered on open spikes.
FOLIAGE 1½ to 5 inches long, lance-shaped, with lobed, wavy margins, developing at the bottom of the plant.
HEIGHT 8 to 22 inches.
BLOOM TIME April and May.
GROWING CONDITIONS Average, fertile, well-drained soil in full sun.
NATIVE LOCATION Southern Europe.

Shepherd's purse is another winter annual, germinating and developing in the cool temperatures of autumn. It rests through the winter then develops and flowers rapidly. Each plant can produce up to 40,000 seeds. That should catch your attention. In early April, Dutch push hoeing will knock the small plants aside, getting to them before they begin active growth. In autumn the density of the perennial planting should have created a closed community, limiting the light that reaches the dormant seeds, inhibiting germination. Another weed you have worn out!

Garlic mustard *(Alliaria petiolata)*

FLOWER Small, white, about ½ inch across, in tight clusters topping each stem.
FOLIAGE Oval to heart-shaped, toothed, 1½ to 4 inches long and wide, in whorls around vertical stems, four to eight stems per plant.
HEIGHT 15 to 34 inches in bloom.
BLOOM TIME May and June.
GROWING CONDITIONS Moist to average, well-drained soil in all shaded areas.
NATIVE LOCATION Europe.

This unique plant, prized by some in Europe as a cooking herb, was introduced here for the same reason and has now seeded itself from coast to coast, crowding out natives. A cool-season biennial, it produces hundreds of seeds per plant. First-year plants are small rosettes of foliage, remaining green through the winter. They seed around in mid-July through August.

Garlic mustard begins active growth in March; watch for the foliage to perk up. At this time, if you have large amounts of bed space taken up by this weed, hire a professional horticulturalist or restoration specialist. They can spray glyphosate and kill the garlic mustard without harming other plants that are below the soil. Now, replace the weed with a long-lived community that covers the earth (think carex!). Your job is to give the new plants the advantage; let them bind together, creating a closed community and limiting the opportunity for garlic mustard to have a home. The replacement plants will begin keeping the garlic mustard at bay while you grab the Dutch push hoe. As the population of garlic mustard declines, keep whatever is left from seeding. If you can't pull them out, cut them down. Keep the seed down. With well-timed persistence, you *can* wear the plant out.

Pennsylvania smartweed
(Polygonum pensylvanicum)

FLOWER Numerous, dense, white to rose-pink spikes, arching slightly at the top of stems.
FOLIAGE Glossy, lance-shaped, 2 to 4 inches long.
HEIGHT 34 to 48 inches in bloom.
BLOOM TIME Mid-June into October.
GROWING CONDITIONS Moist to dry, disturbed soils (ditches, cultivated fields, gardens) in full sun.

NATIVE LOCATION Eastern North America.
Although its seeds are relished by all kinds of wildlife, this weed is another reminder that not all native plants receive an enthusiastic garden welcome. It appears quickly when the weather warms up in June, the stems and foliage growing with ease between the desired garden plants, especially in moist gardens with high organic matter. Smartweed can escape the hoe when it's close to the garden perennial, making it a common sight during the summer months of "observational weeding." It is easily spotted when it begins flowering and is pulled effortlessly from the ground; the roots give way freely.

Horseweed *(Conyza canadensis)*

FLOWER Greenish white clusters of very small florets on long stalks, creating an open panicle atop the plant.
FOLIAGE Light green, linear, 1½ to 3 inches long, developing crowded on the stems.
HEIGHT 26 to 38 inches in bloom.
BLOOM TIME Mid-July into late October.
GROWING CONDITIONS Prefers and does best in dry soils and full sun.
NATIVE LOCATION North America.
This persistent native plant may not be garden-worthy or -welcome, but it sure does make tough situations green, showing up in almost all urban open lots, as well as in cultivated fields, roadsides, pastures, and most gardens. The foliage blends in well with the perennials, but when the plant begins to flower,

it's very noticeable—one of the main objectives of "observational weeding" during the summer months—and is easily pulled.

Annual fleabane
(Erigeron annuus)

FLOWER Round-topped panicles of small, white to light pink daisies, about ¾ inch in diameter.
FOLIAGE Lower leaves are oblong, getting linear at the base; they dry up when the plants are in bloom. The upper stem leaves are toothed, lance-shaped, 1 to 6 inches long, medium green.
HEIGHT 24 to 48 inches in bloom.
BLOOM TIME Mid-May into late October.
GROWING CONDITIONS Moist to dry soil in full sun.
NATIVE LOCATION North America.
This plant is found everywhere open woods, meadows, hay fields, gardens—and not a bad look for empty lots within the city. It can germinate and establish in the fall and begin flowering right away in May. Seeds ripen quickly. If you don't get to this weed with some urgency and it seeds, the soil seed bank will build up and plants will continue to appear at a heavy rate. The seeds that develop the year before should quickly be eliminated by hoeing in May. Again, some of the plants may have been too close to the garden perennials; you'll definitely take notice when they flower get them out as soon as you can.

Plants (and other tools) vs weeds

One goal of the Know Maintenance approach is to have the garden plants provide 50 to 75% of the total weed suppression. Truly, your plants are capable of this; you'll just have to join in with a few contributions to the cause, at timely moments.

The manufacturers of weed barrier fabric and especially the chemical companies want you to believe you are at war with weeds. Their goal is to sell you a product, and they want you to buy it over and over. According to them, there's no other option. But, whether mats or chemicals, traditional products used over and over in the same location damage the health of all the living beings in the soil. The Know Maintenance approach is a much more reasonable alternative. The processes I'm going to describe to you will encourage fresh thinking that can only benefit your plantings.

Getting a competitive edge over weeds does not have to be a war; all you need to do is outsmart them and accept that a certain amount of work will be needed to accomplish your goal. Gardening should consist of knowledge-based work, and it should be enjoyable—you should perform very few truly burdensome tasks. You should be doing things because you want to, not because you have to!

First, you need good tools, which is where the Dutch push hoe comes in. Why is this tool so good? You don't need to bend over when using it. A standard agricultural hoe works only when you bend one-third of the way over, which places tremendous stress on your lower back. You wind up spending as much time resting and rubbing your back and stretching as you do hoeing weeds. In contrast, the Dutch push hoe allows you to stand perfectly upright. As you hoe, you are energetically moving forward through the garden, not pulling. The cutting blade fits perfectly between the plants. This stress-free, upright movement also lifts you emotionally—you're accomplishing so much more at a faster pace, it's truly difficult to stop. I might seem overly enthusiastic, but for 27 years I cleaned our gardens either stooped over an agricultural hoe or crawling through the gardens on hands and knees with a weeding knife. That was 27 years of unnecessary labor.

Here's a timetable for keeping weeds at bay. Remember that weed seeds are persistent and will continue to germinate throughout the growing season wherever sunlight falls on open soil. But the efficiency of the push hoe and the style of planting will combine to help you outwit the weeds.

Carex flacca and *Allium angulosum* 'Summer Beauty' weave together, doing two things simultaneously: greatly reducing opportunities for weeds and welcoming you to autumn.

- Season 1. In spring or after the initial planting, grab your Dutch push hoe and work it in between and around every plant. You will need to do this every 14 to 20 days, at which stage the germinating weeds will usually be 1 to 2 inches tall. You should be able to hoe each 140-square-foot garden plan in roughly 14 minutes. It's important to be consistent—if you are, then the germinating seedlings will lose the opportunity to compete.
- Season 2. Hoeing at 14- to 20-day intervals should continue in the second season. Remember—this is when the plants are developing and growing into their mature stage of life. Once the plant community matures, your initiative will have paid off and the time you spend hoeing will be reduced.
- Season 3 and beyond. You have now moved from the nurturing stage to the establishment stage, and your routine will change accordingly.

After the gardens are cut back in early spring, observe when small weed seeds begin germinating. Also look for winter annuals like chickweed and shepherd's purse that did not get removed last fall—they should be handled quickly. Sharpen that blade and start hoeing! After the

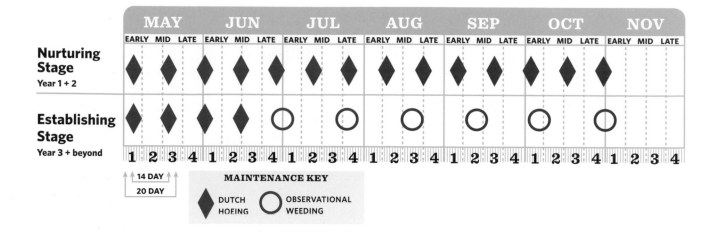

initial removal of the winter annual weeds, you may have 14 to 20 days before the soil temperature warms up for summer weeds to begin germinating. If you have a lot of winter annual weed seeds in your soil, they will continue to germinate and you'll need to stay after them.

From early May (and possibly earlier, in some regions and seasons) through mid-June you need to pursue germinating weed seeds between the developing perennials. Again, this will consist of hoeing the garden every 14 to 20 days, depending on the volume of weed seed germination. If you keep the planting clean, the perennials will fill in, creating a closed plant community by mid-June. This tightly knit community will aid you in reducing the weed population, eliminating sunlight from reaching open soil and thus greatly inhibiting weed seed germination.

By about late June and continuing through the season, the planting will become so tight that you can no longer do any hoeing, so you will switch to what I call "observational weeding." Your initial effort during this period will be determined by how well you kept the weeds managed in spring. The small ones you missed or that germinated within a plant or right next to the developing crown will now have become larger and very visible, so you gently move about the planting, pulling them out by hand. By early July there will be some fairly large chickweed and henbit deadnettle snuggled in between some perennials, but the majority of visible, vertical weeds will be sow thistles. By late July and August the majority of visible weeds will be foxtails. Observational weeding takes agility and care as you gently walk within the plants, reaching, pulling, and carrying the weeds about. I enjoy the casual and limited time I spend doing this—it gives me a sense of interaction with the plants and allows me to observe their developing relationships with one another.

During the season, much of your weeding effort will be focused on transitional areas, where beds meet pathways or where two different plant communities meet, because weed seeds germinate where light reaches open soil. You'll need to keep hoeing, based on the rate and volume of weed seed germination; again, this may be as often as every 14 to 20 days. Keep a crisp, clean-cut edge in these areas. The eye will see it and embrace the tended transition from garden to path. You should edge your planting areas two times during the season: right after you cut back the perennials in spring and then again in July.

Sometimes a weed will appear in the center of a plant, or will hide so you don't see it, so that it reaches a size that requires more than an energetic pull. In these situations your best ally is a durable weeding knife. In particular, be on the lookout for that triple threat: Canada thistle, quackgrass, and field bindweed. These must not be allowed to persist! Dandelions aren't quite as pernicious, but you should still try to eliminate them—you don't want them going to seed. Hoeing, and the closed community of perennials, will help keep the dandelions from gaining a toehold. Persistence wins!

Watering your established planting

By the third season, the planting should be established, and your watering practices too will change from the nurturing stage discussed in the previous chapter. Your observations and practices will be geared to the characteristic soil moisture needs of the plant community and monitoring the rainfall during the growing season. The garden plans in this book generally will need only moderate supplemental watering, having most of their shared water needs met by average seasonal rainfall. You should keep track of rainfall events during the season, so you'll know when and how much to water.

A word of warning: don't rely on programmed irrigation

systems. The majority of these systems are programmed by the installation team, who believe everything has the same requirements as turf and will grow the same height. This practice is just wrong! Each planting has its own soil moisture requirements.

Here's how to water the garden plans in this book. First, get to know the monthly rainfall averages in your area. Generally there is sufficient soil moisture and rain in April and May. Keep track of actual rainfall during these two months; this will give you a good beginning to relate to weather patterns and have an awareness of the amount of rain you received. Usually, additional water is not needed until June.

To maintain your planting at a high-quality aesthetic level, the planting should receive a total of 5 inches of water in June, July, and August. If rainfall in your area doesn't supply that much, then the difference should be made up by as many 1-inch irrigation applications as necessary. The idea is to apply 1 inch of water only as needed in between rain events. By tracking the amount and frequency of rainfall and applying water as necessary, you are much more in tune with the process. You are no longer just the laborer in the garden, showing up "just because"—you are directly connected to your garden's growth, actively engaged in nurturing it, but only as needed. You could even say you're having fun!

Reading the level of soil moisture in relation to your plants' appearance is a skill that will come in time. It's deeply satisfying to know when your planting is in need of water, and—with equal clarity—to know when it is not. Challenge the wastefulness of irrigating everything four times a week for 15 to 20 minutes at four o'clock in the morning! Water use should be thoughtful and should be in your hands. Here are some thoughts on how—and how not—to irrigate.

- Don't install drip irrigation. This system is practical if you're growing linear rows of vegetables, but when you try to weave the hose around all your perennials, the spacing is often too close and at the same time too far from other plants throughout the garden. This creates areas that are quickly wet while other locations stay dry. The water is not distributed equally to all plants. Plants placed within the grid communities of this book's garden plans were chosen because they have similar soil moisture needs. These needs become difficult to meet by meandering drip hoses through the garden. It's frustrating and costly. Also, it has a uniquely bad appearance.
- Do install an impact sprinkler on a sturdy tripod—a much better alternative. Try to find one that's well

made; some are constructed of thin aluminum and fall apart as soon as you begin to use them. Also, get a simple timer that you can place on the end of your water source. Usually these timers can be set for two hours. You can then turn your sprinkler on and go do something else. If you don't remember it's on or get too busy with another project, the timer will shut your water off. You can relax.

- If your garden becomes larger and you feel you need in-ground sprinklers, make sure that (1) you can change the risers as the plants get bigger; and (2) you have control over the system. You should be able to determine when the sprinklers are on, for how long, and how often.
- Use rain gauges to determine how much time it takes to get 1 inch of water from your sprinkler and how evenly the water is distributed throughout the garden. Place three or four rain gauges at different distances from the sprinkler, then let it run for an hour and see how much water is in each gauge. Because the water won't be evenly distributed by the sprinkler, you may need to add slightly more than an inch to one area to receive an inch within the sprinkler's entire range. Note the time needed to get 1 inch of water.
- Be aware that, during summer, the morning dew reduces water loss from the plants for a brief portion of the day. Not only that, it is collected by the narrow foliage of shorter grasses and runs down their blades into the soil, constituting a sort of natural watering process—nothing approaching the volume and scale of the former prairies, but it's nice to know your plants are doing what they can to contribute to the garden's success.

Plant dynamics in the garden

Above and beyond the basic elements of care and maintenance is the practice of enhancement—that is, some sort of alteration in your planting (presumably for the better). One aspect of enhancement is driven by the plants themselves; we can call this plant dynamics. The contributing factors to this natural process include the reseeding of some plants within the planting, the development of plants as they mature, and their interaction with other plants within the garden. The other aspect of enhancement is dependent entirely and actively on you, the result of your continual evaluation of the garden. Perhaps you feel a need to refine and balance your planting, adding

The dynamics sparked by modestly reseeding volunteers can create some of the nicest combinations. This *Echinacea purpurea* seeded into the plant community from another area, actually adding value to the composition and illustrating that sometimes your best contribution to the garden is to let your plants have some immunity from the hoe.

new textures, structure, or colors. You may see a space that needs more height, or that should have more blue in June, less yellow in July, or a more grass-like texture in September. Enhancement gives you the opportunity to be an artist. It is amazingly rewarding to feel you've successfully enriched your garden.

Plants are never static—their stems, foliage, and flowers emerge, develop, and expand. Plant dynamics is simply the ability of plants to move around within the garden. Do you need to prevent this from happening? Not at all! Some of your most beautiful combinations will happen by chance. You're looking for, anticipating, and discovering change; it's up to you how much variation you'll allow. Each time you're in the garden, you will have new views and emotional responses to the plantings. That's good! You're a big part of the dynamics.

If you worry about reseeding, don't. Many of the plants featured in this book do not reseed or do so modestly. Remember—you're in charge. If you see seedlings, you decide whether they add or subtract value to the planting. On occasion you will surprise yourself by allowing something to develop just to see what the new combination might be. Another aspect of plant dynamics is the development of plants through the season and over a period of years. Your response to their maturation will influence the cultural practices you use to maintain their health and their relationship to the entire planting. There is no specific moment when a plant overcrowds a neighboring plant or has to be divided.

Remember, these community plantings are meant to live closely with each other. With this intimacy, some plants may weaken and disappear over time—and that might be fine, as long as the whole of the planting maintains its beauty. Plants don't need to be protected from one another—allow them to blend together. If you see a plant that is getting crowded out, you can move it into another spot or let the dynamics unfold. As long as the overall health and aesthetics are sound and you understand the direction the planting is headed, you will stay as relaxed as the garden.

Here are a couple of examples of plant dynamics in the garden, along with some possible responses. Let's assume that 60% of an area has been planted with *Amsonia* 'Blue Ice' and 40% with *Sesleria autumnalis*. The amsonia has short, spreading rhizomes that push persistently through the soil. The sesleria is a clump-forming grass. Very soon, the amsonia will begin to crowd into the crowns of developing clump grass. In three years, the seslerias will be small, appearing not to have grown very much, because the amsonia has reduced their potential to reach mature size.

At this point the planting will have a dense habit, but the grass influence will be subtle. You have choices. If you like it, you can simply let it be. Or, as you see this look developing in the third year, you could remove some of the amsonia and add more sesleria, making the combination heavier on the grass side. If you prefer the original balance between the wider amsonia foliage and the sesleria, you can remove some amsonia rhizomes each year, allowing the crown of the sesleria to mature and thus maintaining the integrity of the initial design. As the sesleria gets wider and stronger, it will be better able to hold off the amsonia, so you won't have to thin the rhizomes as frequently (but you'll still need to pay attention).

Here's another scenario. Let's assume a planting of 60% *Calamagrostis ×acutiflora* 'Karl Foerster', a clump-forming, vertical grass, and 40% *Coreopsis verticillata* 'Grandiflora', which spreads by short, persistent rhizomes. You'll notice after the third season that the coreopsis is being pressured by the calamagrostis: although its rhizomes are advancing through the soil, their progress will be halted when they reach the calamagrostis, which by this point will have developed into strong clumps. During the fourth season and beyond, keep evaluating the planting. If you want fewer showers of golden yellow flowers and more early season, vertical greenery, simply increase the amount of calamagrostis. Or it could all just be fine.

Situations similar to these two "garden run-ins" will occur with every pattern you plant. Be aware that your gardening time can be affected by the plant combinations you create and the various needs the plants have beyond basic care. Managing the stability of your combinations directly relates to choices you make.

Reviewing your design

It's a good idea to make yourself a list of questions when you review your designs. Here are some possibilities:

- How much additional water beyond rainfall will I need to maintain the health of this planting?
- Are there any plant combinations that will give me additional work? If so, will I be able to commit to the extra work?
- Do I have enough early bulbs in the planting to accent the developing perennials?
- Do I have moments of color through the season, or have I singled out one portion of the season for strong color?
- Do I have too many reseeding plants?

The handsome globular seedheads of *Allium cristophii*, which were added one year after the rest of the planting, add strong architecture to this lakeside vignette. Enhancement is ongoing; being satisfied is too boring. Really, what garden ever really stops? Like great works of art, they are never finished, only abandoned.

- Will the soil be covered quickly early in the season by the developing plants to minimize weed competition?
- Have I paid enough attention to light conditions throughout the year?
- Do the plants I'm placing next to one another have compatible growth rates?
- What plant groupings will I have to keep a close eye on to manage their slightly aggressive growth habits?
- How do I keep from having too much fun?

Dividing plants

You will most likely need to remove portions of plants to maintain the health and artistic style of your plant communities. These small divisions of plants can be replanted in thoughtful ways:

- You can develop a garden nursery area for your small divisions, and as they become larger, you can add them to existing garden sites or give them to friends and family, or the local garden club.
- Don't feel obliged to grow on every single division. If you still have leftovers after planting some and giving some away, the best solution is to compost them. If you keep saving them and planting them on your property, in a short time you'll have a one-note garden dominated by only those plants.
- Many of the plants called for in the garden plans can be re-established in your nursery area and used in newly designed garden spaces. You can develop your own source of plants for future projects and even hold your own neighborhood plant sale.
- Remember, as you re-establish the new divisions,

to employ the nurturing practices described in the previous chapter. Be mindful of possible competition from surrounding mature plants.

Dividing plants is easy—almost too easy. But it does take energy! You need to have a good breakfast and a sharp tile spade: this time, its narrow shovel head is helpful in limiting disturbance to neighboring plants. Here are some simple plant-dividing principles:

- Keep your tile spade filed, so it will easily move through the soil and the crown of the plant you are dividing.
- The best time for making divisions is April and early May, when the plants are just emerging from the earth. At this stage, the new growth is very small and they will not have used up much energy.
- Dig the entire plant out of the ground; the root ball should be proportionate to the size of the crown of the plant—it doesn't have to be huge. It's all right if the soil falls away and roots are exposed. Be calm. The plant will live!
- To make multiple divisions, lay the freshly dug plant on the ground and place the tile spade firmly on the middle of the plant. Steady the shovel, then use your foot to push the shovel through the root ball. You now have two plants. If the root ball is big enough, you can make even more divisions.
- Your divisions should be no smaller than your fist—that way, they will re-establish swiftly.
- When planting the divisions, remember to water them in heavily and place leaf mulch around them to keep the soil evenly moist. In spring they will begin rooting strongly in four to six weeks. Keep an eye on them,

Stand back and squint: you can see the *Penstemon digitalis* 'Husker Red' has been seeding around. What "notes to self" would you make? Do you resolve simply to pull any new penstemon seedling that pops up? Or would you remove some penstemon and add something else? When would you do this—now, in the fall, or next spring? Would you add a completely new component or more of something already present? You'll have such thoughts as long as you garden

water well initially, and water thoughtfully as they re-establish. Please don't go out and purchase any commercial rooting products or fertilizers—you don't need them.

- Your plants can also be divided from mid-September into mid-October, but you'll need to make sure the divisions are sizeable. When you replace the soil around the division, firm it thoroughly, making sure to reduce the air spaces around the roots, then water heavily and place 1 to 2 inches of leaf mulch around the plants. The rains will usually keep the soil moist after your initial watering, but if the weather is dry, you'll need to do additional watering—just don't keep the soil overly wet.

Adding new styles

Another aspect of garden dynamics comes into play when you feel the need for change, for whatever reason. This is your artistic choice—the intimate connection between self-awareness and self-expression. Don't listen when others say, "Oh, but it looks so good—why go to all that work?" Trust yourself, make the change. You're doing something because you're learning. Keep moving forward—your relationship to art and gardening are being forged.

Let's look, for example, at the first of the pair of garden plans inspired by van Gogh's *Poet's Garden* (page 138). After the third or fourth year, you begin to feel there's too much sesleria. Although the garden is beautiful, the look is too grassy for your taste. You could remove a few seslerias and add two or three 'Ostfriesland' salvias, blending some vertical purple into the white 'Schneehügel' salvia. This is gardening!

Another garden change may be enlarging the bed. When you do this, study the immediately adjacent plant groupings, then add plants that relate to them. If you're unsure what to add but you believe the bed needs to be larger, simply add more of the same plants (divide what you have planted) after enlarging the bed. Take your time to think over what else you might like to add—and do it when you're ready. Remember, work at your own pace.

As every planting evolves, you'll have many opportunities to make small changes—perhaps just rounding the bed's corners—but do them patiently at first. Many gardens are now changed over too quickly; people feel they are not being entertained soon enough. The plants can only grow at *their* own pace and are best judged in two to three years. When you garden patiently, the changes you make come from a deeper sense of beauty and knowledge.

The ongoing healthy life of your garden depends on you. The simplest requirement is to be consistent. If you garden in a consistent manner, the plants will live well, the combinations will continue to evolve, and the definition of what makes something beautiful will be clearer to you.

Keep revisiting and reviewing the design questions listed earlier as you introduce new plants and plant patterns. You want all your new plants and patterns to fit well into the existing garden. You want to make sure you understand the effects any changes will have on the care and maintenance of the planting, so you are not doing more than you're capable of. Above all, you always want to keep your gardening time manageable and joyful. As you come to know the plants better, your creativity and the reality of gardening will slowly come together.

Chapter 5

Key Plants for Know Maintenance Gardens

The plants profiled in this chapter are featured in the garden plans of chapter 6. I've selected them primarily for dependability: they are suitable to the northern half of the United States; they live especially well in the soils and climate of my region (northern Illinois, southeastern Wisconsin) and are proven successful north into Minnesota, east into New York, west into Iowa, and south into Missouri. Each plant has an adaptable nature with regard to seasonal weather changes and soil, and most will thrive even with minimal understanding and attention from the gardener. They have the patience to live nicely for a while, giving you time to come to know them better; as your knowledge of each plant develops, the health and style of your garden will grow.

These formal plant entries are ordered alphabetically by the plant's botanical name, since this aids communication and avoids possible confusion about which plant is meant. For example, if you were looking for Penstemon digitalis any place on earth, from France to Japan, you could be reasonably sure of getting the right plant. In contrast, if you were to ask for beardtongue, you might get any one of more than 200 species of penstemons (to say nothing of the hundreds of cultivars). It's the same way with people: when you know both their first and last names, it's the first step to developing a solid friendship. Even though I've included the plants' most widely used common names, you should get in the habit of using botanical names.

Next comes a simple description of the flower or collective flowers. When you actually see the plant in bloom, your knowledge will deepen. The information given for foliage will give you some idea of its appearance and structure: its size, shape, color, and arrangement on the stem. Get to know this part of the plant well, especially its change from late spring to autumn and its decline in winter.

Knowing the plant's seasonal growth rate is a very important part of working in a community, so often two ranges of height are given. Likewise, there are two time frames relating to the spread of the plant after initial planting; it takes five years for most perennials in this book to reach their maximum width. Bear in mind that as they reach maturity, they will be tightly mingling with their neighbors, which is the intimate beauty we are all after. As you guide the planting through time, you may need to thin the crown or divide some plants to redefine relationships.

The plant's typical season of bloom, from beginning to finish, is also given. Most plants will reach their maximum height during this time.

Growing conditions are critical. No one can put a plant in the ground without some advance consideration of the physical world the plant wants to live in. The information in this category is very straightforward. I have used the phrase "average, well-drained soil" almost as a mantra. But even if you believe you don't have this ideal soil, don't give up—even neglected soil in suburban areas can heal rapidly, and when nurtured well after planting, this old scarred earth offers a strong, increasingly healthy home for plants. With a thoughtful beginning, the plants, earth, and gardener will all live well together.

However, abandoned city lots and newly constructed but poorly engineered planting spaces may have soil that is even more deeply damaged—plants put into this kind of soil, which is anything but "average," often simply linger and die. If you find yourself in this difficult situation and are going to do a planting, revisit chapter 3 before planting.

It's all about site preparation where young plants are concerned, and with proper preparation and good nurturing, you'll be able to provide a continually better ecology.

Frequently an entry includes my suggestion for a combination of two plants, a "first date." I specify the percentage of each plant to use so you can mingle them together, creating a small community. You can incorporate this group into your existing garden, if the combination can live well with your present site conditions and the competitive nature of the existing plants. It's a simple good start!

Each formal description concludes with my personal observations. These remarks have their origin in my love of the plant and the practice of conscientiously watching, learning from, and understanding it as it lives from moment to moment. This habit of continual observation is essential; for example, if you know a lot about the flower but little about what happens to the plant in wet weather, the overall well-being of your garden will suffer. Each of you will find your own level, your own practice, gaining value from it and sharing that language with others. I hope that when you experience and learn new and varied responses from a plant, you'll get in touch with me. Let me know how plants live in your region and planting situation. In time, this kind of communication will encourage the development of true plant practitioners—responsible, purposeful folks who lightly tend more beautiful yards and gardens.

Plants for sun or shade

Many of the perennials and grasses in this chapter require sun, but not everyone has that. In extending the Know Maintenance system to shady areas, I wanted to avoid filling the garden with hostas. I realize their strengths, which includes their ability to reduce weeding, but a planting dominated by hostas seems so limiting and uneventful. Similarly, I've seen gardens filled with native woodland plants (*Dicentra canadensis*, *Sanguinaria canadensis*, *Aquilegia canadensis*, *Uvularia grandiflora*), and by early summer there were too many empty areas with garlic mustard meandering through. And of course everyone complains about a lack of color—they have too much shade and can't do anything. Shade gardening has always been a challenge, but some folks have approached it with undeniable panache. I believe they all have something in common: they view shade as a beautiful resource, something we should consider ourselves fortunate to have. When a person realizes they have a special place, that it's not just space to fill with random elements, then the shade garden becomes its own place of beauty. Color takes on a different meaning; texture welcomes harmony; and tones of green are no longer boring.

I now approach shade gardening with the same energy I devote to sunny gardens. As with the communities of sun-loving plants, the aim is to cover the ground with lasting plants that can limit maintenance and live together stylishly and well, and that can be enhanced, as time permits, with selections that match your site conditions and will live well with the established plants. The plants I have selected for the nine garden plans for shade are forgiving of reasonable changes in their habitat. We all have to keep finding new beauty—that's the only way our gardens and landscapes will evolve beyond wood chips.

The special role of sedges

Recalling the natural associations in remnant woodlands, I began to understand the relationship between community planting and healthy shade gardens. I saw in woodlands the same connective lifestyles I found in the prairie. The most eye-opening discovery I made was the life-giving presence of sedges, members of the genus *Carex*. They covered the woodland floor, building healthy soil. They created dense plantings yet lived harmoniously with other plants, sharing space with all the spring wildflowers, ferns, shrubs, and trees. They are all about mixed company! Once you are familiar with sedges and understand how they behave, you will find them invaluable for shade plantings. They will be an important part of our new planting styles.

Many sedges are native species that no one in the horticultural industry is growing because there is no demand. Sure, there are some variegated ones, and others with yellow foliage; the uniqueness of their leaf color contributes to their entertainment value on the sales bench. Unfortunately, many of these striking plants are hardy only to zone 7 and above, which means that in colder parts of the country, their use is limited to containers. The hardy sedges, by contrast, aren't overly dramatic on the sales bench or in a garden setting. They are relaxed plants in shades of green and of various heights, shapes, and textures. Many have appealing scatterings of small spikes of upright, drooping, or nodding flowers that appear above or within the foliage in May and June. To most people they look like grasses, but they actually have distinct physical differences in the flowers, stems, and foliage. So

why are they so important? Why should we get to know and understand these grass-like mounds of pleasing, persistent textures? Where do they live? Who do they live with? How do they live? And how do they add value in the garden?

Here in Wisconsin and Illinois they are found in almost every native habitat, from fens, wet prairie, and wet woods to dry prairie and dry woods and everything in between. That's quite a range, and many of the species found in one situation live well in another. Because of their frequency in each habitat, they are large contributors to the overall health of the soils, benefiting all the other plants they live with and creating the fabric for diverse plant communities. The density and volume of their roots, living and dying constantly through the years, as well as their decaying foliage at the end of the season, contribute to the constant yearly balance of organic matter.

You still have to make cultural decisions, selecting the sedge that will live best in the conditions you have. Once you've done that, you can turn to your role as the artist in the garden, placing the plants to develop rhythmic patterns and tonal changes of foliage color to enhance the other plants they are living with. I have developed a few carex grids in this book to get you started, using the plants as a ground layer. Such a planting accomplishes two objectives. First, it creates a closed plant community to minimize agricultural weed competition; second, it allows compatible plants to live within the planting—a contemporary look that can be used in open shade situations and around trees and shrubs.

Come to know the sedges in all their diversity. You will find your interest continues to grow as you find more and more spaces in which they can be used, creating beauty and reducing yearly mulching and weeding.

"I can't grow anything—it's too shady!" Don't think like that. Shade is a resource, not a handicap. One of the simplest groups of plants on earth loves shade and has been patiently waiting for us to join them in that love: ferns. Many native ferns and their cultivars are ready and waiting for you to discover the character and interest they'll add to your shade garden. As you keep finding, knowing, and planting both ferns and sedges, your sense of shade may be redefined. Rather than a challenging place, impossible to cultivate, a shady site becomes a welcoming sanctuary, a spot of quiet calm that stirs and restores you.

Bulbs

No planting is complete without bulbs. In spring, the beauty of early bulbs highlights the textural emergence and development of the perennials. And summer bulbs accent and harmonize with the perennial communities of which they are a part. In April, as the perennials are just emerging, the bulbs will already have spread their foliage over the open soil and begun flowering. Week after week, a variety of bulbs will continue to grow and flower; then as the perennials begin to cover the soil and flower, the bulbs will have finished their cycle of flowering and go dormant, storing the nutrition they require to repeat their performance next spring. Don't be in a hurry to clean up old bulb foliage. Allow the emerging perennials to cover the remnants of the bulbs and enjoy the bulbs' seedheads as they drift within the garden. As the artist in the garden, you can prune out any seedhead that detracts from the garden's appearance.

In April and May, as you watch your plantings develop, you will notice more areas in the garden that could be planted with bulbs. All that space has value. Patiently observing your garden, you will understand the rate of growth of your perennials beginning in March (the day you cut them back) until they cover the earth by mid-June. Take some pictures in spring so you know where your bulbs are and where some new ones could be planted in autumn. Keep everything in balance. Don't rush; let the knowledge come to you. Another good idea is to plant bulbs in an evaluation area; there's no better way to know them than to live with them. If you want to understand bulbs in a deeper way, consult the recommended reading section for some good books.

The bulbs singled out in this chapter are fun to grow, easily planted, and great mixers, which is why they are called for in the next chapter's garden plans; but many other bulbs could be incorporated into all the grids and additional plant communities you create. Keep trying different ones, focusing on the species bulbs: they have the genetic ability to share space well with the emerging perennials. Over-hybridized bulbs often become too tall, too quickly, have foliage that can cover up emerging perennials, and flowers that are too big: it's all about them! In contrast, species bulbs have lived for generations sharing space with other plants—with them, and with every plant in the A-to-Z listing that follows, it's all about the collective "us"!

Achillea 'Hella Glashoff'
(yarrow)

FLOWER Rounded and flat, 2 to 3½ inches in diameter, soft yellow, maturing to a creamy yellow to white, then a beautiful dark brown.

FOLIAGE Dark green, fern-like, 3 to 7 inches long.

HEIGHT 10 to 14 inches in late spring, 24 to 30 inches in bloom.

SPREAD 10 to 12 inches in two years, 16 to 18 inches in five years.

BLOOM TIME Mid-June into mid-July, the flowers maturing and changing color into late August.

GROWING CONDITIONS Average, well-drained soil in full sun, lean conditions. Frequent mulching and irrigation will shorten the life of this and all achilleas.

FIRST DATE Achillea 'Hella Glashoff' 30% / Allium angulosum 'Summer Beauty' 70%

Nice vertical/upright growth habit, the stems are very strong. The wonderfully rich green foliage combines too well with the soft yellow flowers. Do not prune the flowering stems off until you cut the entire plant back in March. All plants living around 'Hella Glashoff' are enhanced by the color shifts of the flowers as they mature, and the plant's upright structural beauty. In soils that have higher percentages of organic matter, the plant may need to be divided every four to six years. Another achillea that requires little effort from you is Achillea 'Coronation Gold', and a larger, bolder plant is A. 'Gold Plate'.

LEFT The strong stems of Achillea 'Hella Glashoff', lower right, are a vertical presence into December. This substantive character keeps the plant involved artistically in the garden community.

RIGHT Agastache 'Blue Fortune' is a butterfly magnet.

Agastache 'Blue Fortune'
(giant hyssop)

FLOWER Spikes of lavender-blue, 3 to 5 inches long, closely covering the top of the plant.

FOLIAGE Deep green, an oval ending in a point, 2 to 3½ inches long, developing densely on sturdy, slightly leaning stems.

HEIGHT 8 to 14 inches in late spring, 32 to 38 inches in bloom.

SPREAD 12 to 16 inches in two years, 18 to 26 inches in five years.

BLOOM TIME Late July into mid-August.

GROWING CONDITIONS Average, well-drained soil in full sun.

FIRST DATE Agastache 'Blue Fortune' 30% / Echinacea purpurea 'Rubinglow' 70%

The upright flowers in mid- to late summer are beautiful and easy to blend with other perennials and mounding grasses that reach their maximum height just below. The late emergence from the earth in May creates a good planting opportunity for bulbs. During July and August, agastache will maintain a vibrant appearance if you provide 1½ to 2 inches of water to the planting each month, in addition to average rainfall. In early October, the plant begins to turn yellow-green and then (quickly, depending on how low temperatures get) to a rich dark brown, providing fall and winter character.

Allium angulosum 'Summer Beauty' (ornamental onion)

FLOWER Round, 1½ to 2 inches across, lilac, held 5 to 6 inches above the foliage.

FOLIAGE Glossy, rich green, ⅜ inch wide, develops in tight clumps, slightly arching.

HEIGHT 8 to 10 inches in late spring, 16 to 18 inches in bloom.

SPREAD 8 to 10 inches in two years, 12 to 14 inches in four years.

BLOOM TIME Late June into early August.

GROWING CONDITIONS Average to slightly drier, well-drained soil in full sun to light shade.

FIRST DATE *Allium angulosum* 'Summer Beauty' 40% / *Sesleria autumnalis* 60% The flowering stems have a burgundy-yellow fall color; the lower foliage has yellow fall color; the plant has a vertical/mounding growth habit. Most importantly, this allium does not reseed. 'Summer Beauty' mingles nicely with many plants having similar growth rates, offering endless opportunities to develop new plant patterns. Lives well on average rainfall. Cut back in March; by that time, most of the stems and foliage have broken apart, and it would be easy to leave the plant debris scattered around the plants.

LEFT *Allium angulosum* 'Summer Beauty' with a shot of *Echinacea* 'Pixie Meadowbrite'.

RIGHT If it's a showstopper, it must be *Allium atropurpureum* in June.

Allium atropurpureum

FLOWER Maroon-purple, 2½ inches in diameter, oval to slightly flattened look from the side view.

FOLIAGE ¼ inch, narrow, flat, about 15 inches long.

HEIGHT 20 to 28 inches in bloom.

BLOOM TIME June into early July.

GROWING CONDITIONS Average, well-drained soil, full sun.

Excellent vertical/upright growth habit. The flowers are held high aloft on strong stems, above the emerging foliage of surrounding perennials. Very enjoyable look, not commonly found in American gardens. The maturing seedheads appear as clusters of floating green marbles through the summer. This plant is the poster child for communal planting it lives well with and enhances all its fellows. Plant one or two bulbs together and drift them unevenly through the garden.

Allium caeruleum (*A. azureum*)

FLOWER Round, 1½ inches across, soft blue.

FOLIAGE Narrow, ¼ inch wide, medium green, 12 to 16 inches long.

HEIGHT 20 to 24 inches in bloom.

BLOOM TIME June.

GROWING CONDITIONS Average, well-drained soil, full sun.

Too nice! The easy blue spheres float above and through the foliage and flowers of all the garden plants in June. You can scatter these bulbs, creating rhythmic patterns through your planting. This allium will reseed but doesn't inhibit the development of established garden plants. Don't fail to add it to any plant community in sun.

Allium carinatum subsp. *pulchellum* (summer allium)

FLOWER Small, open-rounded, purplish pink.

FOLIAGE Narrow, rounded, green, 12 to 14 inches long.

HEIGHT 14 to 18 inches in bloom.

BLOOM TIME Late July into August.

GROWING CONDITIONS Average, well-drained soil, full sun.

This bulb adds very nice vertical growth and explosions of little flowers arching above and through the perennial garden plants. It can reseed but in diverse plantings does not interfere with the lifestyle of other plants it comes up in the spaces between them. Alternatively, try *Allium carinatum* subsp. *pulchellum* f. *album*; it has all the same characteristics except with white flowers.

Allium cristophii (star of Persia)

FLOWER Large, round, 8 inches across, a globe of small, starry, violet florets.

FOLIAGE 5 to 7 inches long, lax, strap-like, medium green.

HEIGHT 12 to 16 inches in bloom.

BLOOM TIME Late May into late June.

GROWING CONDITIONS Average, well-drained soil, full sun.

Knowing the growth rate of surrounding plants will help you place this bulb to best advantage; its impressively large, round flowers offer a sharp contrast to most. Even the lime-green flower buds are exciting. The maturing flower heads are dark brown and look nice in the summer. Plant one or two together, then scatter them through the garden. They will reseed, which could work out fine; if they are not where you like, hoe them out—you can't miss their unique early foliage. In May, you're Dutch-push-hoeing anyway!

LEFT The soft blue flowers of *Allium caeru leum* leave viewers speechless.

CENTER In bloom, *Allium carinatum* subsp. *pulchellum* looks like fireworks going off!

RIGHT *Allium cristophii* is just right. It looks comfortable amid emerging perennials, flowering just above their foliage.

Allium flavum

FLOWER Small, open-rounded, butter-yellow, clustered.

FOLIAGE Narrow, rounded, blue-green, 12 to 14 inches long.

HEIGHT 14 to 18 inches in bloom.

BLOOM TIME Late July into August.

GROWING CONDITIONS Average, well-drained soil, in full sun; does well in dry conditions.

Here is a great allium to interplant with any number of plants, especially short grasses. It's bluish foliage creates a good contrast to the greens of surrounding plants in early spring and the soft yellow flowers of this "early bulb" are the surprise of summer, floating in the air just above the other plants. In a few years, seedlings will appear. That's ok the reseeding alliums will not inhibit the perennials and will continue to add color to the garden. If you have enough in one site, dig them out and replant them in other dry gardens. Lives well on average rainfall.

The soft yellow of *Allium flavum*'s flowers drifts between the open stems of *Molinia caerulea* subsp. *caerulea* 'Poul Petersen'.

Allium moly (lily leek)

FLOWER 2-inch rounds of yellow florets.
FOLIAGE Bluish green, ½ to ¾ inch wide, pointed, arches over as the flowering stems develop.
HEIGHT 10 to 14 inches in bloom.
BLOOM TIME Late May to mid-June.
GROWING CONDITIONS Average, well-drained soil, full sun.

This allium is easily blended with grasses that are shorter early in the season, giving the impression the grasses are blooming bright yellow. Looks great with *Sesleria autumnalis* or *Sporobolus heterolepis*. The stiff, soft blue foliage provides a nice tonal and textural contrast to the shades of green developing in May. In July the flower heads are light brown and slowly disappear as the garden plants mature into August. You could plant 15 to 20 per 10 square feet.

Amsonia 'Blue Ice' (bluestar)

FLOWER Purple-blue, star-shaped, in clusters.
FOLIAGE Linear-ovate, 1 to 2 inches long, medium green, developing quickly through May into a dense, layered plant.
HEIGHT 10 to 12 inches in late May, 12 to 18 inches in bloom.
SPREAD 8 to 12 inches in two years, 18 to 22 inches in four to five years.
BLOOM TIME Mid-June into mid-July.
GROWING CONDITIONS Moist to slightly dry average soils in full sun to light shade.
FIRST DATE *Amsonia* 'Blue Ice' 40% / *Allium angulosum* 'Summer Beauty' 60%

Amsonia 'Blue Ice' has a mounding growth habit and spreads by very short rhizomes. Foliage stays clean during the growing season, turning greenish yellow in fall. The plant enjoys its own company, growing into itself very comfortably and filling space nicely, which means it thrives in larger groups within the garden community. In a few years, depending on location or companionship, the rhizomes could be thinned out. Lives well on average rainfall once established and surprisingly well in moist soil that dries out slightly in summer. This one's easy to use and appreciate!

LEFT The bright yellow florets of *Allium moly* awaken the emerging green of perennials and the soft, early developing grasses.

RIGHT *Amsonia* 'Blue Ice' combined with the light, rounded lavender flowers of *Allium schoenoprasum*.

Amsonia tabernaemontana var. salicifolia (willow-leaved bluestar)

FLOWER Light blue, star-shaped, ½ inch wide, in clusters to 4 inches across, carried at the top of the stems.

FOLIAGE Narrow, ovate, about 3 inches long, medium green, develops tightly on stems mainly in June, post-flowering.

HEIGHT 28 to 36 inches in late spring, 34 to 42 inches in bloom.

SPREAD 16 to 20 inches in two to three years, 32 to 40 inches in five years.

BLOOM TIME Early to mid-June.

GROWING CONDITIONS Average, well-drained soil in full sun to light shade.

FIRST DATE *Amsonia tabernaemontana var. salicifolia* 20% / *Echinacea purpurea* 'Rubinglow' 80%

In early spring the developing stems are blackish gray, a beautiful contrast for mid- to late April bulbs. The plant grows quickly in May, and after flowering begins vegetative growth, reaching its seasonal width and height by early to mid-July. It has a vertical/mounding growth habit and lives well in its own company; with that last characteristic and its rapid seasonal development, it's a good plant in modest groups for season-long weed suppression. The foliage stays clean during the growing season, then turns a bright yellow in fall. Lives well on average rainfall.

The soft blue flowers of *Amsonia tabernaemontana* var. *salicifolia* complement the emerging, light green foliage of *Coreopsis verticillata* 'Grandiflora'.

Anthericum ramosum is a summer
pleasure, its small white flowers
dancing above the foliage.

Anthericum ramosum
(St. Bernard's lily)

FLOWER Spikes of open, starry white
flowers, ½ to 1 inch wide.

FOLIAGE Narrow, grass-like,
grayish green.

HEIGHT 14 to 18 inches in late spring,
28 to 32 inches in bloom.

SPREAD 8 to 14 inches in two years, 16
to 18 inches in five years.

BLOOM TIME Mid-June into mid-July.

GROWING CONDITIONS Average, well-
drained soil in full sun.

FIRST DATE *Anthericum ramosum* 40% /
Sesleria autumnalis 60%

This useful plant is not at every garden
center; you'll need to track it down. It
has a clumping vertical/upright, grass-
like habit, with open, airy, flowering
stems. In late August the seedheads
can get messy; do some "artistic pruning" to remove the declining flowering
stems. The foliage turns yellow-green in
autumn, later having no winter interest.
Anthericum lightly reseeds; remove any
seedling that disrupts the style of the
evolving garden community. This inspir-
ingly soft-textured plant lasts and lasts;
once established, it will live well on average rainfall.

Asarum canadense (wild ginger)

FLOWER Cup-shaped, maroon with white center, ½ to ¾ inch wide and 1 inch long. Found between the ground-level stems of the plant, hugging the ground.

FOLIAGE 5 to 7 inches long, 4 to 6 inches wide, heart-shaped, slightly velvety to the touch yet with a leathery, shiny look. Especially beautiful emerging from the ground in April the leaves are closed, a dusty silver-white, then they open—fresh and medium green. Very energizing!

HEIGHT 6 to 10 inches in late spring and in bloom.

SPREAD 9 to 14 inches in two years, 16 to 20 inches in five years.

BLOOM TIME April into late May.

GROWING CONDITIONS Average, well-drained to moist soil; very adaptable but does not do well in constant dry conditions, where it will linger prettily, then decline and die.

FIRST DATE *Asarum canadense* 40% / *Carex flacca* 60%

Here is a neat groundcover plant that's durable, yet it shouldn't go it alone the plant is deciduous, disappearing quietly by late October. The flowers are under the foliage; they're not going to be seen unless you get right down on the ground, but they are definitely interesting enough to make it worth the trip. Asarum covers the ground early and boldly, and its beauty is lifted when it's with other plants. Planted from 4½-inch pots with carexes, it develops into a good shade garden carpet that will inhibit weed development. You can enhance the planting as your time allows.

RIGHT The large leaves of *Asarum canadense* are a bold contrast to most other plants.

LEFT Behind the *Amsonia tabernaemontana* var. *salicifolia* are the architectural purple-gray flower spikes of *Baptisia* 'Purple Smoke'.

Baptisia 'Purple Smoke' (false indigo)

FLOWER Pea-like, ¾ to 1 inch, pale purple-gray, carried in spikes, becoming great brown/black seed pods in late summer.

FOLIAGE Compound leaflets, dense composition, very textural, bluish green.

HEIGHT 26 to 32 inches in late spring and in bloom.

SPREAD 14 inches in two to three years, 25 inches in five years.

BLOOM TIME June.

GROWING CONDITIONS Average, well-drained soil in full sun.

FIRST DATE *Baptisia* 'Purple Smoke' 20% / *Echinacea purpurea* 'Dwarf White Swan' 80%

Everyone appreciates this one in the garden. Beautiful, purplish green, smooth stems emerge in mid-April. Very structural plant, developing a vertical/mounding growth habit. Lives well on average rainfall. In fall the foliage turns black and dies away nicely don't rush to cut it back; enjoy its decline into winter. Get it established and enjoy the beauty.

Baptisia sphaerocarpa
(yellow false indigo)

FLOWER Spikes of bright yellow, ½- to ¾-inch, pea-like flowers.

FOLIAGE Compound leaflets, blue-green, very textural.

HEIGHT 28 to 36 inches in late spring and in bloom.

SPREAD 14 to 18 inches in two years, 22 to 28 inches in five years.

BLOOM TIME June.

GROWING CONDITIONS Average, well-drained to dry soil, full sun to light shade.

FIRST DATE Baptisia sphaerocarpa 30% / Geranium sanguineum 'New Hampshire Purple' 70%

Attractive, bluish stems emerge in mid-April, combining well with Narcissus 'Jetfire'. Develops a vertical/mounding habit in mid-June. Exuberant yellow flower spikes cover the plant when it's in bloom, then new vegetative growth mingles with the developing black seed pods. Baptisia is a great structural element in the garden and refreshingly more blue tone than green. In fall the plant turns brownish black. Don't rush to cut it back; enjoy the casual complexity and beauty of change. This is another plant that lives well on average rainfall.

Calamagrostis ×acutiflora 'Karl Foerster' (Karl Foerster grass)

FLOWER Loose, narrow, purple-tinged spikes, maturing to a soft tan.

FOLIAGE Rich green, sturdy, vertical.

HEIGHT 26 to 40 inches in late spring, 55 to 72 inches in bloom.

SPREAD 12 to 16 inches in two years, 18 to 24 inches in five years.

BLOOM TIME Smooth, soft purple in late June, tan-colored by early August.

GROWING CONDITIONS Slightly moist to average, well-drained soil in full sun to part shade.

FIRST DATE Calamagrostis ×acutiflora 'Karl Foerster' 40% / Coreopsis verticillata 'Grandiflora' 60%

This grass combines very early, rapid development in April with a dynamic vertical/upright growth habit. The early growth is upright then slightly arching, then the vertical flowering stems take off. Easily adds an architectural style to the garden. Provides early-spring enthusiasm, complementing all the new growth of other perennials and bulbs that have and will bloom. Cut back to 5 inches in mid-March. Calamagrostis lives well on average rainfall. It's an enjoyable but overworked plant for the last quarter century, these grasses have welcomed mall shoppers and bank customers from the Mississippi River to the Atlantic Ocean. This beautiful plant should be used more thoughtfully, appreciated for its strong constitution and compatibility with so many plants.

LEFT Baptisia sphaerocarpa, a tireless contributor.

TOP RIGHT Calamagrostis ×acutiflora 'Karl Foerster' standing strong behind Nepeta subsessilis 'Sweet Dreams' and Perovskia atriplicifolia 'Little Spire'

BOTTOM RIGHT The maturing flower spikes of Calamagrostis ×acutiflora 'Karl Foerster' are both a late summer highlight and a welcome to autumn.

Calamintha nepeta (catmint)

FLOWER Very small, white, borne in spikes above the foliage, changing to a soft blue in late September, early October.

FOLIAGE ½ inch, round, glossy, rich green, densely clustered.

HEIGHT 4 to 6 inches in late May, 16 to 22 inches in bloom.

SPREAD 12 to 15 inches in two years, 16 to 20 inches in five years.

BLOOM TIME Late July into mid-October.

GROWING CONDITIONS Average, well-drained to dry soils in full sun.

FIRST DATE *Calamintha nepeta* 40% / *Sesleria autumnalis* 60%

Great textural plant whose mounding growth habit mingles nicely with many plants. The rounded, glossy foliage is a nice contrast to the flat matte greens of other plants—helpful in creating tonal changes in the garden. One happy characteristic is the plant does not reseed. It is a clump grower and respects its space. Where it's planted is where it stays. This is an easy plant to enjoy and introduce to your gardening friends. Calamintha attracts a large number of diverse bees. In late October and November, foliage turns dark brown. Through the winter the plant breaks down; it's easy to prune back and leave the debris around all the plants. Lives well on average rainfall once established.

Camassia quamash (common camassia)

FLOWER Deep blue spikes, 3 to 5 inches long.

FOLIAGE Narrow, shiny, 8 inches long, develops in a dense basal mound.

HEIGHT 10 to 16 inches in bloom.

BLOOM TIME Late May into June.

GROWING CONDITIONS Adaptable, moist to average soil in part shade to full sun; not a plant for dry conditions.

Another bulb whose grassy foliage blends right into the community. Its beautifully vertical shot of early color mingles so nicely with diverse groupings, the only challenge about using it is to first consider all the opportunities it presents. Depending on what it's planted with, you may want to remove the faded flowers.

TOP LEFT In mid-September *Calamintha nepeta*'s clouds of white flowers mix with the maturing seedheads of *Allium angulosum* 'Summer Beauty'.

BOTTOM LEFT By mid-November, calamintha turns medium brown, maintaining its structure, still adding value to the *Sesleria autumnalis*. Both plants provide uninterrupted beauty and pleasure through the season.

RIGHT *Camassia quamash* is an elegant stunner and one of the more unusual early bulbs.

Carex brevior (fescue sedge)

FLOWER Rounded, fuzzy green fading to brown, about ¼ inch in diameter, three to four clustered at the top of the stem. Twelve to 20 flowering stems per plant.

FOLIAGE ⅛ to ⅜ inch wide, somewhat upright, soft green.

HEIGHT 14 to 22 inches in late spring and in bloom.

SPREAD 8 to 12 inches in two years, 14 to 18 inches in five years.

BLOOM TIME Late April to early June.

GROWING CONDITIONS Moist, average, well-drained to slightly dry soil in full sun to part shade.

FIRST DATE *Carex brevior* 40% / *Stachys officinalis* 'Hummelo' 60%

A very pleasant carex with a very forgiving nature, as its requirements for moisture and light attest. The nice upright, slightly arching foliage does not get too dense; it's just right to soften almost any shade plant combination. In December the lower portion of the foliage is green, the upper, soft brown. You will find this plant to be a good selection for many future plantings. Prune it back in March and leave the debris around the plants.

Carex bromoides (brome sedge)

FLOWER Loose, gentle spikes, 1 to 2½ inches long, arching over when they bloom, having a silvery green look. As the seeds mature, they change to a light brown.

FOLIAGE Very narrow, graceful, ¹⁄₁₆ inch wide, soft green, developing densely from the base of the plant.

HEIGHT 10 to 15 inches in late spring and in bloom.

SPREAD 12 to 14 inches in two years, 15 to 19 inches in five years.

BLOOM TIME Late April into late May, nice seedheads into early July.

GROWING CONDITIONS Moist to average soil, in light shade to part shade. It does not do well in dry conditions; the plant will linger, then die.

FIRST DATE *Carex bromoides* 60% / *Veronica* 'Eveline' 40%

Beautiful soft texture! The foliage emerges in April very stiff, brush-like, growing much more relaxed May into June. This plant does not do well in dry soil in July and August; average soils with an eye on some additional water in July and August will keep it healthy. Many textural and color tone combinations can be created with this sedge, and its light brown seedheads are a subtle punctuation to all shades and textures of green. Foliage remains greenish yellow into the winter. Prune back in March and leave the debris around the plants.

LEFT *Carex brevior* has a soft, gentle texture. Using this plant is too easy—think of the possibilities.

RIGHT *Carex bromoides* covers a shaded area gracefully, living well with other plants.

Carex flacca (blue sedge)

FLOWER Slender brown spikes, 1 to 2 inches long, upright at first then gently nodding over, scattered about the top of the plant.

FOLIAGE An engaging bluish green, about ⅛ inch wide and reaching 20 inches long, developing loosely, layering over itself, forming a nice mound.

HEIGHT In late spring, in average to fertile soil, 12 to 14 inches in sun, 8 to 12 inches in part shade; in bloom, in average to fertile soil, 14 to 18 inches in sun, 10 to 14 inches in part shade.

SPREAD 12 to 16 inches in two years, 18 to 26 inches in five years.

BLOOM TIME Mid-June into mid-July, maturing and remaining artistically interesting into mid-September.

GROWING CONDITIONS Average, well-drained soil in full sun to part shade; does well in dry conditions.

FIRST DATE *Carex flacca* 30% / *Sesleria autumnalis* 70%

This sedge has a beautiful soft blue, mounding growth habit, but it does spread by rhizomes and can challenge other plants for space. Be thoughtful when you design! If you use Carex flacca in small amounts, adding tones of blue to the garden, it will not outcompete but rather enhance its companions. It is a good plant that enjoys its own company, so it will live well planted with itself in larger plantings; then it is up to you, as the artist in the garden, to learn what bulbs will mingle and share space well with it. Cut back in mid-March, and the new foliage will develop tightly, with a rich blue early color. Lives well on average rainfall once established. This sedge is a good example of the relationship between site conditions and plant development demonstrating how giving some plants can be to their location. Not much different from us!

The soft blue of *Carex flacca* echoes and highlights the *Allium angulosum* 'Summer Beauty' in this light shade planting.

Carex grisea covers the ground with rich, dark green foliage in late October; in mid-February, it's just as green.

Carex grisea (wood sedge)

FLOWER Green, ¾- to 1-inch spikes, at the top and along the sides of the flowering stems. As the seeds mature, the flowering stems lean over. The new vegetative growth in June grows through the brown seedheads.

FOLIAGE Dark green, ¼ to ½ inch wide, smooth, flat, developing densely from the base of the plant.

HEIGHT 9 to 14 inches in late spring and in bloom.

SPREAD 9 to 12 inches in two years, 14 to 18 inches in five years.

BLOOM TIME Mid-May into mid-June.

GROWING CONDITIONS Average, well-drained soil in light shade to part shade; does well in moist soils in spring that dry out going into summer.

FIRST DATE *Carex grisea* 70% / *Hosta* 'Niagara Falls' 30%

This dependable, attractive plant is one of the main sedges to include in an average-soil shade garden, and yet it's highly unlikely anyone you know has used it in their shade garden. Its beautiful rich green, narrow foliage lasts through the winter and is very tolerant of changes in soil moisture. *Carex grisea* will reseed in open areas, filling gaps within the planting and under shrubs nicely. Remember, your first task is to develop a community of plants that live well together and inhibit the germination and competition of weeds. Such a "carex community" is the best beginning for your shade garden, and this native carex is patiently waiting for us all to figure out what it has to offer.

Carex montana
(mountain sedge)

FLOWER Yellow to brown with maturity, ¾- to 1½-inch spikes, clustered at the top of the flowering stems, covering a good portion of the plant.
FOLIAGE Rich, bright green, ⅟₁₆ to ⅛ inch wide, fine and firm, linear, upright to arching, forming stocky clumps.
HEIGHT 15 to 22 inches in late spring and in bloom.
SPREAD 10 to 12 inches in two years, 14 to 18 inches in five years.
BLOOM TIME Early April into late May.
GROWING CONDITIONS Moist, average, well-drained to slightly dry soil in full sun to part shade.
FIRST DATE *Carex montana* 70% / *Carex flacca* 30%

You have only to look at the growing conditions to see this native European sedge is a durable plant that lives in diverse habitats. That amenable cultural characteristic makes *Carex montana* one of the many plants necessary in all designed gardens, a plant of continuity. Prune back just above the new growth in March; leave the debris in the garden around all the plants. Seed ripens and falls in July, but I have not seen any reseeding in my gardens in the four years I have had it. Lives well on average rainfall. As the plant ages, it loosens up in the center as the rhizomes spread outward; when it creates this loose ground layer, other plants can fill in the spaces as they appear. You can choose which plants to add or manage the ones that have moved in on their own. There will always be something to do! It's like breathing you will do it all your life—you just don't want to worry about it.

Carex montana **is a plant of continuity, one that creates repetition and harmony in a garden.**

Carex pensylvanica in April bloom, a carpet of small yellow flowers just above its emerging foliage.

Carex pensylvanica
(Pennsylvania sedge)

FLOWERS ½- to 1-inch spikes. The bright yellow stamens of the male flowers are atop the flowering stem; the brown female flowers are just below.

FOLIAGE Deep green, ⅛ inch wide, developing a semi-dense, tufted look; in late August the top third turns light brown.

HEIGHT 8 to 12 inches in late spring and in bloom.

SPREAD 10 to 12 inches in two years, 14 to 18 inches in five years.

BLOOM TIME Early April into early May.

GROWING CONDITIONS Dry to average, well-drained soil, light shade to part shade.

FIRST DATE *Carex pensylvanica* 60% / *Carex montana* 40%

Too easy. Here is one of many plants we have discussed that lives well on average rainfall and offers a way to return open space to long-term health. This is a good carex to plant initially it covers the ground effectively, yet other plants co-exist peacefully with its spreading rhizomes. In bloom, visual interest is high it looks like a meadow of yellow Q-tips. This carex should be one of the main ground-layer plants when planting a sloped, shaded area. Great, appealing plant—many plant combinations would be enriched by it, but we need to always use it thoughtfully.

Carex shortiana (Short's sedge)

FLOWER 1- to 1½-inch-long, ¼-inch-wide spikes, stiff, developing atop and alongside the stems, olive-green in bloom changing to dark brown.

FOLIAGE ¼ to ⅜ inch wide, medium green, flat, forming dense clumps.

HEIGHT 15 to 22 inches in late spring and in bloom.

SPREAD 8 to 10 inches in two years, 12 to 16 inches in five years.

BLOOM TIME May to late June.

GROWING CONDITIONS Moist to average soil in full sun to part shade.

FIRST DATE *Carex shortiana* 40% / *Eurybia divaricata* 60%

A nice architectural carex, it adds a soft-textured green element to the planting. The dark brown flower spikes float within the foliage, really standing out through the summer months, remaining a presence into September. In late September, the foliage turns soft yellow—pretty nice. Cut this sedge back in March and leave the debris around the plants. It grows quickly through May, filling garden space rapidly. Lives well on average rainfall. Simply, it's a good plant!

Carex sprengelii (Sprengel's sedge)

FLOWER Silvery green, narrow, in spikes about ¼ inch wide and 2 inches long, approximately four spikes per stem and 10 to 14 stems per plant, drooping over at bloom time.

FOLIAGE ⅛ to ¼ inch wide, medium green, 24 to 30 inches long, forming dense clumps.

HEIGHT 14 to 18 inches in late spring and in bloom.

SPREAD 10 to 14 inches in two years, 16 to 20 inches in five years.

BLOOM TIME Late April into late May.

GROWING CONDITIONS Moist to average, well-drained soil in full sun to light shade.

FIRST DATE *Carex sprengelii* 40% / *Geranium* 'Orion' 60%

This is a beautiful architectural plant in April and May—upright, arching foliage and clusters of drooping, narrow flowers just above. A Disney moment. Now to its other side. In mid-June, most of the flowering stems lie down; this opens up the center and new vegetative foliage emerges, filling the center of the plant by mid-July. When they are planted in large groups, the floppy appearance in June is messy. So, the best way to use this carex is to place a few throughout the planting, as accents. It then becomes a good team player. It will also seed within your planting; thin out the seedlings as they disrupt the garden style, or leave them if they are an enhancement to their new location. Prune back in March and leave the debris around the plants. Lives well on average rainfall.

LEFT *Carex shortiana* has a nice upright, slightly arching growth habit, but the highlight is the green flower spikes that turn dark brown in mid-summer—truly an outgoing characteristic.

RIGHT *Carex sprengelii* in October, its now-golden flower spikes catching the early light.

Carex swanii (Swan's sedge)

FLOWER Short, thick spikes, about ¼ inch wide and ⅝ inch long, green as they begin to flower, changing to medium to darker brown into July.

FOLIAGE Narrow, ⅛ inch wide, slightly hairy, medium green, develops densely from the crown of the plant.

HEIGHT 14 to 18 inches in late spring and in bloom.

SPREAD 14 to 16 inches in two years, 18 to 20 inches in five years.

BLOOM TIME Early May into mid-June.

GROWING CONDITIONS Average to well-drained soil in full sun to part shade.

FIRST DATE *Carex swanii* 40% / *Salvia nemorosa* 'Wesuwe' 60%

You will enjoy this carex—its soft, restful texture, its gentle, arching habit, the insignificant yet very visible, small flowers—all highlight and enliven other perennials within the planting. Stays green going into November. Cut it back in March. Lives well on average rainfall once established. Can create continuity within the garden. Always think about the potential!

Count *Carex swanii* as another "carex for continuity" in the garden.

Chionodoxa forbesii (glory of the snow)

FLOWER Six-petaled "star," blue with a white center, arranged in clusters on the stem.

FOLIAGE Narrow, ⅜ inch, medium green, developing at the base of the plant.

HEIGHT 5 to 8 inches in bloom.

BLOOM TIME Late March into early April.

GROWING CONDITIONS Average, well-drained soil in full sun to part shade.

If you are going to cut back the garden with a mulching mower, this bulb is invaluable it is the first to bloom after the garden has been cleaned up each March. People are unaccustomed to seeing plant debris left in the garden and feel it looks messy. In two to three weeks when the chionodoxa begin flowering, their blue flowers make the light brown plant debris look perfectly placed. I have used 15 to 20 chionodoxas per 10 square feet. They seed easily and begin to fill empty areas. So far I have found this to be alright; they have not inhibited the perennials, since they develop so early in spring.

Chionodoxa forbesii **is also the "glory of the cut-back garden," every March.**

Coreopsis palmata
(stiff coreopsis)

FLOWER Yellow-gold daisies with a darker center, about 1 inch across. The rich green seedheads look like cups; their ¼-inch size makes them very noticeable from mid-summer to September, when they turn dark brown.

FOLIAGE Dark green, interestingly lobed in threes, about 1 inch long, rough to the touch, densely covering the plant.

HEIGHT 14 to 20 inches in late spring, 22 to 30 inches in bloom.

SPREAD 10 to 16 inches in two years, 16 to 24 inches in five years.

BLOOM TIME Late June into late July.

GROWING CONDITIONS Average, well-drained to dry soils in full sun.

FIRST DATE *Coreopsis palmata* 30% / *Sporobolus heterolepis* 70%

This plant spreads by rhizomes; without competition from neighboring plants, it will get too big too quickly. Also you don't need to plant a lot of these together; space one, two, or three together, then another group 8 to 12 feet off. Very delightful flower effect— they do not densely cover the plant but rather are scattered freely over it, allowing the dark green foliage to pop through. The deeply cut foliage stands out against other garden plants as it develops through the season, lending a layered look. In late September, the foliage turns reddish yellow, then dark brown in November. Lives well on average rainfall. *Coreopsis palmata* is little used in ornamental plantings simply because no one has taken the time to get to know it.

Count on *Coreopsis palmata* for a perfectly balanced and contrastful mingling of flowers and foliage.

Coreopsis verticillata 'Grandiflora' effectively complements the early July flowers of *Phlox paniculata* 'Blue Paradise', just behind.

Coreopsis verticillata 'Grandiflora' (tickseed)

FLOWER Golden yellow daisies, 1 to 1½ inches in diameter, clustered densely at the top of the plant.

FOLIAGE Finely divided, narrow, lacy, medium green.

HEIGHT 14 to 18 inches in late spring, 24 to 30 inches in bloom.

SPREAD 10 to 12 inches in two years, 18 to 24 inches in five years.

BLOOM TIME Early July into early September.

GROWING CONDITIONS Average, well-drained soil in full sun to light shade.

FIRST DATE *Coreopsis verticillata* 'Grandiflora' 30% / *Echinacea purpurea* 'Virgin' 70%

This plant has a slightly loose, vertical/mounding growth habit. In fall the foliage turns a beautiful yellow-green, dark brown by November. The long bloom time and soft textural appearance make this plant a strong component of many plantings. Try incorporating it into light shade with some *Hosta* 'Guacamole' and *Carex shortiana*. Surprise people! Unlike many of the recent coreopsis introductions, including the omnipresent 'Moonbeam', this one pulls its weight. 'Grandiflora' lives nicely on average rainfall. Another fine selection is *Coreopsis verticillata* 'Zagreb', which is shorter with a tighter, more compact growth habit.

Dryopteris marginalis
refreshes its delicate, evergreen presence each spring.

Dryopteris marginalis
(leather wood fern)

FOLIAGE Dark green, glossy, lance-
shaped, divided into many leaflets,
evergreen.
HEIGHT 16 to 20 inches.
SPREAD 8 to 12 inches.
GROWING CONDITIONS Average, well-
drained soil, light shade to part shade.
FIRST DATE *Dryopteris marginalis* 60% /
Carex pensylvanica 40%

Texture-rich accent for all shade plantings, but it begins life in your garden
slowly it will take three years for it to
become a healthy-looking plant. This
upright, arching fern remains evergreen
through the winter; the foliage starts
browning in mid-April as the new fronds
emerge from the soil, reaching their
maximum height and spread by early
June. It does not spread by runners like
Matteuccia struthiopteris (ostrich fern),
which is more commonly seen in plantings. Nor does it turn brown in summer like ostrich fern. Lives well on average rainfall once established. As you
do more shade gardening, you will find
yourself placing these and other unde-
manding ferns in combinations with
many plants.

Echinacea purpurea 'Virgin'
(white purple coneflower)

FLOWER 3- to 4-inch-wide daisies, white petals, large golden green cone.

FOLIAGE Coarse, 3 inches wide, lance-shaped, medium green, mainly on the lower portion of the plant.

HEIGHT 6 to 10 inches in late spring, 26 to 32 inches in bloom.

SPREAD 5 to 8 inches in two years, 12 to 14 inches in five years.

BLOOM TIME Early July into late August.

GROWING CONDITIONS Average, fertile, well-drained soil in full sun to part shade.

FIRST DATE *Echinacea purpurea* 'Virgin' 70% / *Agastache* 'Blue Fortune' 30%

One of the best echinacea selections, introduced by Piet Oudolf. The old flowering stems and seedheads turn dark brown and have a great fall and winter appearance. Good stiff stems and vertical/upright structure translate to lots of possibilities: make sure you try a planting in part shade, where it lives well. Short, frequent periods of irrigation during the season will promote rhizoctonia, a fungal disease that affects the crown of the plant, causing the foliage to wilt and the plant to die. Reseeds modestly; remove the seedlings if they interfere with the garden's direction. You're a part of the dynamics, you're the gardener. Some other good cultivars are 'Dwarf White Swan', 'Kim's Mophead', and 'White Swan'. Try planting them mixed together!

Echinacea purpurea 'Rubinglow'
(purple coneflower)

FLOWER 3- to 4-inch-wide daisies, with slightly arching, purple-red petals and dark cone.

FOLIAGE Coarse, 3 inches wide, lance-shaped, dark green, mainly on the lower portion of the plant.

HEIGHT 8 to 10 inches in late spring, 26 to 32 inches in bloom.

SPREAD 5 to 8 inches in two years, 12 to 14 inches in five years.

BLOOM TIME Early July into late August.

GROWING CONDITIONS Average, fertile, well-drained soil in full sun to part shade.

FIRST DATE *Echinacea purpurea* 'Rubinglow' 70% / *Panicum virgatum* 'Heiliger Hain' 30%

This plant invites many combination possibilities, thanks to its nice vertical/upright growth habit. During the flowering period, the stems are various shades of maroon, turning dark brown, along with the old seedheads, for a great fall and winter appearance. Short, frequent periods of irrigation during the season promote rhizoctonia, a fungal disease that affects the crown of the plant, causing the foliage to wilt and the plant to die. Reseeding is a modest characteristic; remove the seedlings if they interfere with the garden's direction. Pot up some of the seedlings; you may come up with some color tones that would enhance your planting. You never know. Some other good selections are 'Fatal Attraction' and 'Dwarf Pink Swan', as well as the regional variations of the species. You all know of the tremendous amount of hybridized echinaceas (the soft pink 'Pixie Meadowbrite' is one I can vouch for). You will need to try these in your region and see if they have the genetic strength to make it.

LEFT *Echinacea purpurea* 'Rubinglow', grown from seed, is much more durable than many coneflower hybrids.

CENTER With its colorful stems, *Echinacea purpurea* 'Rubinglow' doesn't need to be in flower to be beautiful.

RIGHT The rigid white petals of *Echinacea purpurea* 'Virgin' draw a horizontal line between *Agastache* 'Blue Fortune' and *Perovskia atriplicifolia* 'Little Spire'—too nice!

Epimedium ×*versicolor* **'Sulphureum'** (barrenwort)

FLOWER Small, cup-like, ½ inch by ¾ inch, sepals medium yellow, cup darker yellow, held in delicate clusters on thin, strong stems.

FOLIAGE Heart-shaped, about 3 inches long and 2 inches wide, emerging in spring on wiry stems. New growth is subtly tinted in bronze, turning to a leathery, rich green by June, layered very densely, and by autumn, becoming slightly reddish.

HEIGHT 7 to 9 inches tall in flower, 11 to 15 inches in late spring.

SPREAD 8 to 10 inches in two years, 12 to 16 inches in five years.

BLOOM TIME Late April into mid-May.

GROWING CONDITIONS Average, slightly moist to slightly dry soils in light shade to part shade.

FIRST DATE *Epimedium* ×*versicolor* 'Sulphureum' 40% / *Geranium sanguineum* 'Max Frei' 60%

As with daylilies, there are many epimediums you may want to try. One thought is to mix some together—say *Epimedium* ×*rubrum* with *E.* ×*versicolor* 'Sulphureum', for example—and create a mosaic of colors and textures. Why not? It's sad these plants disappoint people whatever their color, however flirtatious their "spurs," the flowers aren't showy enough and don't last long enough for them. Thankfully, the epimediums could care less! They go on living, spreading slowly but diligently; still, space them close— about 15 inches to tighten up in three years. *Epimedium* ×*rubrum*, with pink and white flowers, takes slightly longer to fill in than 'Sulphureum'. In March mow off the old foliage so it doesn't interfere with the quick-growing flower stems in early April. These plants do their vegetative growing after they flower; June is the time they develop new rhizomes. From mid-June into mid-August, if rainfall is limited, give the planting three to four deep waterings.

All epimediums cover ground with stylish grace and foliage that maintains its good looks well into winter. Here is *Epimedium* ×*rubrum*, in bloom.

Eupatorium dubium 'Little Joe', slightly taller than 'Baby Joe', underplanted with *Eurybia divaricata.*

Eupatorium dubium 'Baby Joe' (Joe-pye weed)

FLOWER Purplish pink florets, very bold, gathered in neat, rounded, somewhat dome-shaped clusters above the plant.

FOLIAGE Dark green, lance-shaped, slightly oval, toothed, 4 to 5 inches long, developing in whorls of four to five around the stem.

HEIGHT 8 to 12 inches in late spring, 34 to 42 inches in bloom.

SPREAD 16 to 22 inches in two years, 26 to 34 inches in five years.

BLOOM TIME Mid-August to mid-September.

GROWING CONDITIONS Average, well-drained to moist soil in full sun to light shade; not a plant for dry conditions.

FIRST DATE *Eupatorium dubium* 'Baby Joe' 60% / *Panicum virgatum* 'Heiliger Hain' 40%

'Baby Joe' creates a scene in August, very outgoing plant. Its short height, unique for a eupatorium, means its dense flowers can now relate to another level of plants in the garden. That's exciting— the more relationships you can create, the better and more varied your artistic experiences will be. Eupatorium may need irrigation in dry Julys and Augusts. As you walk through the garden, keep an eye on the foliage; when it starts to droop noticeably downward, a deep watering would be helpful. In late September the plant begins turning medium brown, but its structure remains strong, and the brown flower heads are a seasonal highlight into winter. Cut the plant down to the ground in March. Bulbs are easily planted and live well with it, thanks to eupatorium's late emergence from the earth. A nice taller selection is 'Little Joe', which gets 50 to 58 inches tall.

Euphorbia polychroma 'Bonfire' (cushion spurge)

FLOWER 1 inch, soft green, flat, surrounded by bright yellow bracts (modified leaves), covering 75% of the plant during bloom season.

FOLIAGE ½ to 1 inch, oval, new growth deep purple, red, and orange, turning to light green, on thin stems.

HEIGHT 12 to 14 inches in late spring and in bloom.

SPREAD 12 to 16 inches in two years, 16 to 18 inches in five years.

BLOOM TIME Early May into mid-June.

GROWING CONDITIONS Average, well-drained soil in full sun; does well in drier soils.

FIRST DATE *Euphorbia polychroma* 'Bonfire' 60% / *Salvia nemorosa* 'Wesuwe' 40%

Beautiful and important many-colored foliage that sharpens the appearance of the garden. Anyone who sees this plant wants more of it. It enriches and highlights the medium green colors of other plants in the garden and adds mystery to salvia hybrids; its final color is a dark red, in late September. Keep this somewhat dense, mounding plant in well-drained soil especially in winter. If you keep the soil lean, it lives well; frequent mulching and irrigation lead to rapid decline.

TOP *Euphorbia polychroma* 'Bonfire', just beginning to flower.

BOTTOM In early June, the dark foliage of *Euphorbia polychroma* 'Bonfire' has a job to do contrastfully punctuating the planting's many shades of green.

Eurybia divaricata lives cleanly through the summer, its dark foliage and stems sparking conversation, its simple, white flowers covering the plant.

Eurybia divaricata (*Aster divaricatus*, eastern wood aster)

FLOWERS Small, white daisies, ¾ to 1 inch in diameter, borne profusely.

FOLIAGE Triangular, toothed, dark green, 1 to 2 inches long, developing on wiry black stems.

HEIGHT 2 to 3 inches in late spring, 14 to 20 inches in bloom.

SPREAD 14 to 18 inches in two years, 18 to 22 inches in five years.

BLOOM TIME Mid-September into mid-October.

GROWING CONDITIONS Average, well-drained soil, light shade to part shade.

FIRST DATE *Eurybia divaricata* 60% / *Hosta* 'Inniswood' 40%

Beautiful mounding aster for shade. A highlight is its dark green foliage developing against and supported by the thin black stems—highly complementary to surrounding plants. Lives well on average rainfall once established. The colder temperatures of late autumn cause the stems and foliage to break down, limiting any winter interest. In March, clean the plant up.

Geranium macrorrhizum 'Bevan's Variety' (bigroot geranium)

FLOWER Rounded, five-petaled, magenta-pink, ¾ to 1¼ inches across, densely clustered above the foliage.

FOLIAGE Rounded, deeply lobed, 2 to 3½ inches across, gray-green, very aromatic, dense.

HEIGHT 10 to 14 inches in late spring and in bloom.

SPREAD 12 to 16 inches in two years, 16 to 20 inches in five years.

BLOOM TIME Late May into late June.

GROWING CONDITIONS Average, well-drained soil, full sun to part shade; does well in drier conditions.

FIRST DATE Geranium macrorrhizum 'Bevan's Variety' 40% / Carex grisea

This mounding geranium lives well on average rainfall and with minimal attention, yet it is little used. Once established in a shade planting, it seems to do very well when the gardener is busy elsewhere. In March when you are pruning plants back, be sure not to cut the foliage below the growing points; that would remove the new growth for that season. Irrigation systems and mulched soils usually cause the spreading rhizomes to decline quickly.

Geranium 'Orion' (cranesbill geranium)

FLOWER Lavender-blue, 1 inch, round, flat, in open clusters atop each stem.

FOLIAGE Deeply cut, rounded, medium green, developing densely from the base, where leaves are 3 inches in diameter, getting smaller moving up the plant.

HEIGHT 16 to 24 inches in late spring and in bloom.

SPREAD 16 to 20 inches in two years, 22 to 28 inches in five years.

BLOOM TIME Early June to mid-July, then half the volume into mid-September.

GROWING CONDITIONS Average to moist soil, full sun to light shade.

FIRST DATE Geranium 'Orion' 30% / Echinacea purpurea 'Virgin' 70%

Even though you need to think about supplemental watering during the drier months of summer, this is an entertaining and valuable plant. So many of the larger geraniums, such as 'Johnson's Blue' and 'Brookside', open up and fall to the ground after flowering, whereas 'Orion' continues to bloom all summer and develops new growth, keeping the center of the plant full. No need to prune to the ground in late June. Watering is helpful in July and August, four or five times—water deeply! The foliage stays green into November. 'Orion' enjoys its own company; larger groupings (seven to 20 plants) do nicely.

LEFT In mid-May the foliage of Geranium macrorrhizum 'Bevan's Variety' covers the earth. Learn to use this characteristic to your planting advantage.

RIGHT The lavender-blue flowers of Geranium 'Orion' hovering just behind the daisies of Kalimeris incisa 'Blue Star'—another combination that keeps our eyes open.

Geranium sanguineum 'Max Frei' beautifully backed up and set off by Nepeta 'Early Bird'.

Geranium sanguineum **'Max Frei'**
(bloody cranesbill)

FLOWER Purplish pink, 1 inch, round, spread over the top of the plant.

FOLIAGE Small, deeply cut, 1 inch, rounded, dark green, turning a nice soft red in fall.

HEIGHT 6 to 11 inches in late spring and in bloom.

SPREAD 8 to 10 inches in two years, 14 to 16 inches in five years.

BLOOM TIME Early June into August.

GROWING CONDITIONS Average, well-drained soil, full sun to part shade; does well in clay to gravelly soils.

FIRST DATE *Geranium sanguineum* 'Max Frei' 60% / *Allium angulosum* 'Summer Beauty' 40%

This low-growing selection lives well on average rainfall and maintains a fresh form into mid-November, blooming heavily in June then sporadically through the season. A good characteristic of all the sanguineum geraniums is that they don't decline due to monoculture pressures they can be planted in larger groups and will grow well into each other, without inhibiting the well-being of their fellows. 'Max Frei' is a handy plant to mingle in just such larger groups between smaller groupings of slightly larger mounding plants, such as *Sesleria autumnalis*. The straight species is also good, as are *Geranium sanguineum* var. *striatum* and *G. s.* 'Album'. These are plants of beauty, charm, and persistence.

Geranium **'Tiny Monster'**
(cranesbill geranium)

FLOWER Purplish pink, 1 inch, round, developing over the entire plant.

FOLIAGE Rich green, 2 to 2½ inches, nicely rounded and somewhat cut, developing in layers upon itself.

HEIGHT 10 to 14 inches in late spring, 12 to 16 inches in bloom.

SPREAD 14 to 18 inches in two years, 22 to 28 inches in five years.

BLOOM TIME Very rich flowering from mid-June into mid-July, then lightly into October.

GROWING CONDITIONS Average, well-drained soil in full sun to part shade.

FIRST DATE *Geranium* 'Tiny Monster' 30% / *Nepeta* 'Early Bird' 70%

This geranium has a mounding habit, a long sustained bloom period, and clean, large foliage that maintains its good looks well into early November. One way to use this plant is to place only a few selectively through the garden, for a repetitive look. Another is to group four to eight together en masse, then inter-plant bulb layers for early April and early May as it emerges in spring, there is plenty of opportunity for bulb plantings.

The autumn foliage of *Geranium* 'Tiny Monster' can be appreciated in hundreds of combinations.

RIGHT *Gillenia trifoliata* is a welcome presence in the garden, always enhancing what is seen and how we feel, and offering visual pleasure in multiple ways.

Gillenia trifoliata (*Porteranthus trifoliatus*, Bowman's root)

FLOWER White, delicate, star-shaped, ¾ to 1¼ inches wide, developing in open clusters above the foliage.

FOLIAGE Rich green, narrow, oval, pointed, sharply toothed, in clusters of three, gracefully attached to slender red stems.

HEIGHT 28 to 36 inches in late spring and in bloom.

SPREAD 8 to 12 inches in two years, 16 to 20 inches wide in five years.

BLOOM TIME Early June into mid-July.

GROWING CONDITIONS Average to slightly moist soil in full sun to part shade.

FIRST DATE *Gillenia trifoliata* 30% / *Echinacea purpurea* 'Virgin' 70%

You will probably be the first in the neighborhood to enjoy this beautiful architectural plant. It's received little attention so far, but once present, it won't go unnoticed for long. When the petals fall, the seedheads change to maroon-red. The soil should not get extremely dry; if July and August rains are limited, irrigation would be beneficial, about 1 inch every two weeks. Groupings of three to nine together remain healthy for several years and develop rapidly early in the season, inhibiting weed competition all summer long. Also look for *Gillenia stipulata* it has many of the same characteristics, except in spring its leaves emerge deeply cut, very fern-like. Great early-spring textural look!

Hemerocallis (daylily)

FLOWER Everyone in America knows the shape and appreciates the broad range of colors and color combinations.

FOLIAGE Strappy, blue-green to yellow-green, arching to upright.

HEIGHT 10 to 28 inches in late spring, 20 to 52 inches in bloom.

SPREAD 10 to 16 inches in two years, 14 to 24 inches in three to five years.

BLOOM TIME Early June to late September, depending on the variety. Some good options!

GROWING CONDITIONS Average, well-drained soil, full sun to light shade.

FIRST DATE *Hemerocallis* 'Chicago Apache' 60% / *Rudbeckia subtomentosa* 40%

Commonly planted perennial, lives well under many conditions. Your choices are myriad available cultivars offer a wide range of colors, rebloomers ('Happy Returns'), bloom times, and flowering stem heights. Many have fairly clean foliage through the growing season; others, the foliage is terrible. Each flower lasts but a single day. After flowering, remove the old stem from within the foliage. Daylilies can be used wonderfully well as an accent point in the garden. Place your groupings in select locations, and the planting will respond to their moment in the spotlight.

The bold red flowers of *Hemerocallis* 'Chicago Apache' offer high energy when drifted through a plant community.

Heuchera villosa 'Autumn Bride' (alumroot)

FLOWER White to cream-white, ½-inch florets clustered on open, narrow panicles, 5 to 7 inches long. Ten to 16 flowering stems per plant.

FOLIAGE Soft green, rounded, slightly cut into about seven lobes, 3½ to 5 inches in diameter.

HEIGHT 10 to 14 inches in late spring, 24 to 30 inches in bloom.

SPREAD 12 to 16 inches in two years, 16 to 18 inches in five years.

BLOOM TIME Mid-August to mid-October.

GROWING CONDITIONS Average, slightly moist to well-drained soil, light shade to part shade.

FIRST DATE Heuchera villosa 'Autumn Bride' 60% / Hosta 'Guacamole' 40%

This heuchera is a durable asset for shade plantings; it has great foliage density, creating nice textural mounds, and lives well on average rainfall. Place in larger groups; it enjoys its own company, and the late-summer panicles of white flowers are ready to give added value to whatever is interplanted with them. When cutting heucheras back in March, do not cut the plant below the growing point; that is the area on the stem where you see new growth developing. If you do cut the plant back too low, it will develop weakly, linger for a while, and probably die. Another good heuchera to try in full sun to light shade is *Heuchera richardsonii*, with vertical spikes of small greenish white flowers in early June and wonderful dark green foliage.

LEFT In late August, the flowers of *Heuchera villosa* 'Autumn Bride' finally arrive to complement its strong season-long foliage.

RIGHT The golden green of *Hosta* 'August Moon', an oldie but goodie, enlivens the tonal sameness of shade plantings.

Hosta 'August Moon'

FLOWER Bell-like, pale lavender, 2 inches long, clustered at the top of the stem.

FOLIAGE Heart-shaped, yellow-green, slightly crinkled, 4 to 6 inches long.

HEIGHT 12 to 16 inches in late spring, 26 to 30 inches in bloom.

SPREAD 10 to 14 inches in two years, 24 to 32 inches in five years.

BLOOM TIME Late June through late July.

GROWING CONDITIONS Average, well-drained soil in light shade to full shade; does well in slightly moist or dry conditions.

FIRST DATE Hosta 'August Moon' 30% / Heuchera villosa 'Autumn Bride' 70%

Hostas are architectural, durable plants that love to live long. And there are so many! But don't be tempted to "collect them all" a collection of hostas is interesting only to a hosta collector. The thing is to be more than a collector— be an orchestrator! Create composition, find the hostas that relate to the diversity of plants in your garden. 'August Moon' develops a mounding habit, and its upright flowering stems pleasingly highlight any shade planting combination. Like many hostas, it is easy to grow and has a forgiving nature; but when planted into more sunlight, its foliage burns easily and will look poor by mid-July.

Hosta 'Guacamole'

FLOWER Bell-like, lavender-white, scented, 2 to 3 inches long, clustered in all directions atop each stem.
FOLIAGE Glossy, heart-shaped, 7 to 11 inches long, 6 to 8 inches wide, apple-green with a dark green edge—very classy!
HEIGHT 14 to 18 inches in late spring, 28 to 32 inches in bloom.
SPREAD 14 to 20 inches in two years, 28 to 38 inches in five years.
BLOOM TIME Early August into September.
GROWING CONDITIONS Average, well-drained, slightly moist to moderately drier soil, in light shade to full shade.
FIRST DATE *Hosta* 'Guacamole' 30% / *Carex flacca* 70%

This hosta is very forgiving, adaptable to a wide range of soil and light conditions. It positively enlivens the soft filtered light of shade, but if you plant it where it gets more direct sun, you mustn't let the soil get too dry, or its foliage will decline. Don't be shy using this plant it makes everything around it look good and like it belongs. It's a moderate grower; by the third season, expect its great, high-energy foliage to make a significant impression in the planting.

Hosta 'Halcyon'

FLOWER Lilac-blue, open at tip and narrowing upward, about 2 inches long, arranged openly atop each stem.
FOLIAGE Slightly narrow, heart-shaped, rich blue-green, about 5 inches wide and 6 to 8 inches long.
HEIGHT 5 to 7 inches in late spring, 24 to 28 inches in bloom.
SPREAD 12 to 16 inches in two years, 22 to 30 inches in five years.
BLOOM TIME August.
GROWING CONDITIONS Average, well-drained, slightly moist to moderately drier soil, full shade to full sun.
FIRST DATE *Hosta* 'Halcyon' 30% / *Polystichum acrostichoides* 70%

This is one of the best blue hostas! The layered, mounding habit (foliage is some 18 to 22 inches tall by bloom time) adds a gentle look to a shaded planting, enhancing any number of combinations using sedges, epimediums, geraniums, and ferns. Don't feel too quickly that you're overusing this plant—it's just that nice. In full sun, it will have good foliage into late June, then the light and drier conditions will begin to scorch the leaves. It won't look perfect, but then again, it won't look that bad either.

LEFT *Hosta* 'Guacamole' has fresh green foliage that easily combines with many shade plantings.

RIGHT *Hosta* 'Halcyon' wandering through a planting of *Carex bromoides*, with *H.* 'Krossa Regal' providing the backdrop. The plants used in between hostas give the garden a sense of gladness.

Kalimeris incisa 'Blue Star'

FLOWER Soft blue, ¾-inch daisies, held in moderately dense clusters at the top of the plant.

FOLIAGE Oval-elongated, 1 to 1½ inches long, slightly toothed, medium green.

HEIGHT 14 to 20 inches in late spring, 24 to 30 inches in bloom.

SPREAD 12 to 16 inches in two years, 18 to 22 inches in five years.

BLOOM TIME Late June into late August.

GROWING CONDITIONS Average, well-drained, moisture-retentive soil in full sun.

FIRST DATE *Kalimeris incisa* 'Blue Star' 30% / *Sporobolus heterolepis* 70%

It's a nice plant, not commonly used, reseeds lightly. If you see a much taller kalimeris in your garden, that's a seedling—pull it out (the species can reseed heavily). 'Blue Star' maintains its nice vertical/mounding shape into fall, by which time the foliage has gone from medium green to green/yellow to yellow/brown. The seedheads look like the tops of rusty nails. In July and August, add 1½ to 2 inches of water per month beyond average rainfall to keep this plant performing at a high level.

Limonium latifolium (statice)

FLOWER Very small, lavender, densely clustered on strong, slender, branching stems.

FOLIAGE Large, oblong, slightly undulating, dark green, 6 to 8 inches long, developing close to the ground.

HEIGHT 5 to 9 inches in late spring, 22 to 28 inches tall in bloom.

SPREAD 10 to 14 inches in two years, 18 to 24 inches in five years.

BLOOM TIME Late July into late August.

GROWING CONDITIONS Average, well-drained soil in full sun; does very well in drier conditions.

FIRST DATE *Limonium latifolium* 40% / *Vernonia lettermannii* 'Iron Butterfly' 60%

This enjoyable plant wants little input. It reseeds modestly but is easily identified by its unique foliage; if it wanders, it can easily be scuffed out. Once established, it lives well on average rainfall; in traditional plantings (too much wood-chip mulch, irrigated frequently), it will linger and die. The long dark green foliage in spring is quite nice; the billowing summer flowers are eye-catching and refreshing. As their lavender fades, the maturing seedheads create a soft brown, textural mound—very expressive!

LEFT The daisy is the understood flower shape, and the constellation served up by *Kalimeris incisa* 'Blue Star' is welcomed by everyone.

RIGHT *Limonium latifolium*'s clouds of lavender settle in between the upright flares of *Echinacea pallida*—two good friends, enjoying the day.

Maianthemum racemosum
(*Smilacina racemosa*, feathery false Solomon's seal)

FLOWER Small, graceful, white, in 4- to 7-inch clusters on developing stems.
FOLIAGE Deep green, ovate, 3 to 6 inches long, 1½ to 2½ inches wide, on single stems developing in groups from the ground.
HEIGHT 20 to 30 inches in late spring and in bloom.
SPREAD 6 to 9 inches in two years, 15 to 24 inches in five years.
BLOOM TIME Early May into late June.
GROWING CONDITIONS Average, well-drained to moist soils, light shade to part shade.
FIRST DATE *Maianthemum racemosum* 30% / *Carex pensylvanica* 70%

The seasonal changes of this hard-working architectural plant never fail to excite the shade gardens in which it is sited, and when it is interplanted with carex and hostas, the beautiful characteristics of all plants in the community are uplifted. In April the stems emerge from the ground, casually spaced from each other; they grow quickly in spring and flower just as the new foliage is developing. In September the seeds are enclosed in light red, rounded fruits grouped loosely on the end of the stems, and the foliage changes to golden yellow. In late November the foliage drops off, and the stems maintain an upright/declining appearance into winter. You can count on maianthemum to colonize in seven to 10 years, at which time you can dig out some of the rhizomes in April (they look like white straws) and add them to other garden plantings. This colonizing habit is one of the plant's strengths its continued slow-paced movement into other plants keeps the planting vibrant at a manageable pace. Maianthemum lives well on average rainfall.

LEFT *Maianthemum racemosum* lights up any shade garden.

RIGHT *Mertensia virginica* brings an accent of blue, always a welcome color, especially in spring.

Mertensia virginica
(Virginia bluebells)

FLOWER Bell-shaped, ¾ inch, pale blue, soft pink in bud, hanging in clusters.
FOLIAGE Light green, 2 to 5 inches wide, 4 to 6 inches long.
HEIGHT 16 to 18 inches in late spring, 18 to 24 inches in bloom.
SPREAD 8 to 12 inches in two years, 12 to 18 inches in five years.
BLOOM TIME Mid-April through late May.
GROWING CONDITIONS Average, well-drained to moist soil, full sun to part shade.
FIRST DATE *Mertensia virginica* 20% / *Carex shortiana* 80%

Mertensia can be placed through your planting individually or in small groups, adding moments of blue in May. But be prepared going to seed, the flowers quickly lose interest, and right after flowering the foliage begins to weaken and fade in color, and the plant begins to go dormant, completely disappearing by late June. Armed with this knowledge, you can see that you must place this plant very thoughtfully and consider what will move into the space created by its departure. In the sun, most perennial plants will readily fill the gaps mertensia leaves behind. In the shade, carexes, hostas, and *Geranium macrorrhizum* can grow into the voids. In five to six years, you can dig the mertensia out in autumn (mark the location with some golf tees) and divide the rich brown roots. Place a division back, if needed, into the same location. Parts of the root you leave in the earth will slowly develop into a new plant also. Lives well on average rainfall.

Molinia caerulea subsp. arundinacea 'Transparent' (moor grass)

FLOWER Purplish early, turning medium brown, in narrow panicles.

FOLIAGE Narrow, medium green, in dense clumps.

HEIGHT 6 to 8 inches in late spring, 60 to 72 inches in bloom.

SPREAD 12 to 16 in two years, 22 to 30 inches in five years.

BLOOM TIME Late July into late August.

GROWING CONDITIONS Average, moisture-retentive soil, full sun to light shade.

FIRST DATE *Molinia caerulea* subsp. *arundinacea* 'Transparent' 60% / *Eupatorium dubium* 'Baby Joe' 40%

This gentle grass goes from vertical/ upright to slightly arching in late June, offering a beautiful see-thru effect. Dry soils will limit flowering; to see the full show, water deeply three or four times during July and August. In early October the grass begins turning fiery yellow, and a beautiful seedhead effect is maintained until mid-November. But from late November until March, when the plantings are cut back, this molinia has no substantial winter interest. Note the straight species, which usually is not available in the nursery trade, does reseed.

Molinia caerulea subsp. caerulea 'Moorhexe' (moor grass)

FLOWER Black-purple early, turning medium brown, in narrow panicles.

FOLIAGE Narrow, medium green, developing in dense, vertical tufts.

HEIGHT 6 to 10 inches in late spring, 32 to 38 inches in bloom.

SPREAD 5 to 7 inches in two years, 9 to 11 inches in five years.

BLOOM TIME Late July into late August.

GROWING CONDITIONS Average to moist soils in full sun to part shade.

FIRST DATE *Molinia caerulea* subsp. *caerulea* 'Moorhexe' 40% / *Stachys officinalis* 'Hummelo' 60%

This grass has a great look! Confidently upright/vertical, then slightly arching as the flowers mature—it is the perfect complement to mounding plants. It turns a beautiful yellow-green in fall and maintains its light brown seedheads into mid-November. The flowering stems develop closely together yet can be seen through, functioning as a scrim. If your soil is too dry in July and August, this grass will not flower well; three or four deep waterings in those months would benefit it. Some other good selections of this subspecies are 'Heidebraut' and 'Poul Petersen'.

LEFT *Molinia caerulea* subsp. *arundinacea* 'Transparent' works incredibly well in any planting. When it flowers, the entire garden is transformed and uplifted.

RIGHT *Molinia caerulea* subsp. *caerulea* 'Moorhexe', rising to the occasion. When the flowers begin to bloom, the panicles appear black, thanks to the dark stamens.

Monarda bradburiana
(eastern beebalm)

FLOWER Globular, soft pink, about 2 inches across, one per stem, loosely clustered above the plant.

FOLIAGE Oval to lance-shaped, glossy green, slightly toothed, 2 to 2¾ inches long and 1½ inches wide, developing opposite each other on the stems, which are loosely upright.

HEIGHT 18 to 24 inches in late spring and in bloom.

SPREAD 12 to 16 inches in two years, 18 to 22 inches in five years.

BLOOM TIME Early June into mid-July.

FIRST DATE *Monarda bradburiana* 40% / *Sporobolus heterolepis* 60%

GROWING CONDITIONS Average, well-drained soil in full sun to part shade; does well in drier conditions.

This perennial is easy to grow and easy to enjoy, mingling energetically with other plants. New growth is a very eye-catching maroon, and the leaves just below the flower maintain that color. The pink of the flowers lasts for quite a long time, transitioning the colors of spring into the new blooming moments of summer. The maturing seedheads are beautiful, rounded, light green changing to medium brown, pleasantly contrasting with whatever foliage is about and lasting long into winter. Each season has its value! Lives well on average rainfall once established. Prune it back only in spring.

TOP LEFT In early May *Monarda bradburiana*'s emerging maroon-tinted foliage enhances the rich bulb planting.

BOTTOM LEFT In early June the soft pink flowers of *Monarda bradburiana* are the froth on the drifts of *Sporobolus heterolepis* as the dark maroon of *Allium atropurpureum* floats above all.

LEFT *Narcissus* 'February Gold', a fine representative of that indispensable class, early bulbs.

RIGHT *Narcissus* 'Lemon Drops', accompanied by the emerging foliage of *Gillenia trifoliata*. You see, without bulbs there is no wholeness to the planting; one moment invites the next.

Narcissus cyclamineus (daffodil)

FLOWER Slender, tubular, with sepals slightly pushed back, in a range of colors from deep yellow to white.
FOLIAGE Strappy, ¼ inch wide, rich green.
HEIGHT 10 to 14 inches in bloom.
BLOOM TIME April into early May.
GROWING CONDITIONS Average, well-drained soil in full sun to part shade.

Great to interplant in small groups within perennial combinations. Nice vertical/upright growth habit. Some good choices from division 6 (cyclamineus) are 'February Gold', 'Jack Snipe', and 'Jetfire'. *Narcissus* 'Quail', from division 7 (jonquil), has a look similar to 'February Gold', but its trumpet is shorter. Bulbs should always figure in your garden plan. There's no nicer moment than the initial sighting of green spears after a long winter, followed by eagerly awaited first flowers.

Narcissus 'Lemon Drops' (triandrus daffodil)

FLOWER Soft lemon-white, two to four per stem, usually two stems per bulb.
FOLIAGE Rich green, ½ inch wide, 9 to 12 inches long.
HEIGHT 10 to 14 inches in bloom.
BLOOM TIME Late April into mid-May.
GROWING CONDITIONS Average, well-drained soil, full sun to part shade.

Easy to enjoy! The multiple, lemon-white flowers, carried above the green layers of emerging perennials, awaken a planting like early morning sunlight. Plant these bulbs in groups of four to seven, scattered through the garden. Don't be bashful, and don't space your groups evenly take your cue from the sky and mimic the randomness of cloud patterns. Other good division 5 (triandrus) daffodils are 'Thalia', 'Hawera', and 'Ice Wings'.

Nepeta 'Early Bird' (catmint)

FLOWER Very small, tubular, violet-blue, clustered tightly on sprays of flowering stems just above the foliage.

FOLIAGE ⅜ to ½ inch, round to oval, gray-green, densely developed.

HEIGHT 10 to 12 inches in late spring and in bloom.

SPREAD 14 to 18 inches in two years, 18 to 22 inches in five years.

BLOOM TIME Early May into late June, sporadically into September.

GROWING CONDITIONS Average, well-drained to gravelly soil, full sun.

FIRST DATE *Nepeta* 'Early Bird' 40% / *Salvia nemorosa* 'Wesuwe' 60%

This nepeta has a mounding growth habit one plant covers a large area quickly. Drift it through the garden, allowing it to fill in between different plant groupings. It will maintain a nice shape and continue to flower lightly through the summer. Through the winter, its foliage breaks down quite a bit; simply prune it back in March and leave the debris around all the plants. It can reseed modestly and lives well on average rainfall once established.

A purple haze of *Nepeta* 'Early Bird' joins *N. racemosa* 'Snowflake' in this carex matrix.

Nepeta subsessilis 'Cool Cat' snuggling next to the glossy foliage and seedheads of *Monarda bradburiana*. Orderly and quiet together, summer passes.

Nepeta subsessilis 'Cool Cat' (catmint)

FLOWER Soft lavender, ½ to 1 inch long, openly arranged on spikes at the top and side of the plant.

FOLIAGE Medium green, oval, toothed, 4 inches long at the base, getting smaller up the plant, densely developed.

HEIGHT 10 to 18 inches in late spring, 28 to 36 inches in bloom.

SPREAD 10 to 12 inches in two years, 15 to 17 inches in five years.

BLOOM TIME Late June into mid-August.

GROWING CONDITIONS Average, well-drained to moist soil, full sun to part shade.

FIRST DATE *Nepeta subsessilis* 'Cool Cat' 40% / *Echinacea purpurea* 'Dwarf White Swan' 60%

This nepeta has not been used very often. The plant has a vertical/upright growth habit and long bloom period; as the first flowers fade, new ones develop on the lower stems. It will benefit from four to six deep waterings (say, an inch every two weeks), July through August. As temperatures drop in October, the entire plant turns medium brown but remains upright into January. In March, prune to the ground. 'Cool Cat' presents you with an opportunity to develop continuity in a planting that moves from sun to shade. Another nice selection is 'Sweet Dreams'; it's medium pink. The straight species is taller, 36 to 40 inches, and reseeds more frequently. Try them—see if they fit in with your gardening style.

Panicum virgatum 'Northwind' (Northwind switch grass)

FLOWER Open, airy panicles, coppery tint early, aging to light brown by late October.

FOLIAGE Dark green with a little blue tone, about ¼ to ⅜ inch wide, developing tightly at the base of the plant in spring.

HEIGHT 10 to 16 inches in late spring, 68 to 72 inches in bloom.

SPREAD 14 to 16 inches in two years, 24 to 30 inches in five years.

BLOOM TIME Mid-August into mid-September, the maturing seedheads delicately interesting into mid-December.

GROWING CONDITIONS Slightly moist, average, well-drained soil in full sun.

FIRST DATE *Panicum virgatum* 'Northwind' 40% / *Rudbeckia subtomentosa* 60%

I selected this easy-to-grow grass in 1982 from a group of panicum seedlings collected in Kane County, Illinois—proof positive that the rich diversity of our native perennials will enable us to continually discover durable, artfully exciting plants. Use this plant where you want to establish a distinctly vertical architectural mood. Both its fall and winter appearances are strong. In March, before your bulbs come up, cut it back to about 4 to 6 inches above the ground. 'Heiliger Hain', another good selection of *Panicum virgatum*, has bluish green foliage that turns slightly reddish in August. Also try 'Heavy Metal' and 'Ruby Ribbons'.

LEFT *Panicum virgatum* 'Northwind' has a dense, strongly upright/vertical growth habit and a nice textural look. What will you do with this architectural building block?

CENTER Age hasn't curbed the beauty of *Panicum virgatum* 'Heiliger Hain', an older selection that is little used nowadays, when it's all about what's new.

The saucer-like flower heads of *Parthenium integrifolium* layer like clouds along the horizon all summer.

Parthenium integrifolium
(wild quinine)

FLOWER Flat-topped, rounded clusters, 3 to 5 inches wide, of waxy white florets, grouped openly atop the plant.

FOLIAGE Rich green, 6 to 8 inches long, 3 to 4 inches wide, clustered on the lower portion of the plant. Height 24 to 30 inches in late spring, 32 to 40 inches in bloom.

SPREAD 10 to 12 inches in two years, 18 to 22 inches in five years.

BLOOM TIME Mid-June into early September.

GROWING CONDITIONS Moderately dry to slightly moist, average, well-drained soil in full sun to light shade.

FIRST DATE *Parthenium integrifolium* 30%/ *Echinacea purpurea* 'Rubinglow' 70%

This is a fine architectural plant with four-season interest, a nice strong texture, and vertical/upright habit, slightly opening up at the top. In October the plant starts turning yellow-brown, changing to dark brown in early November. Keep your pruners holstered cutting any part of this plant back before March would be removing moments of beauty. Lives well on average rainfall.

Perovskia atriplicifolia **'Little Spire'** (Russian sage)

FLOWER Small, tubular, in soft panicles of lilac-blue.

FOLIAGE Deeply lobed, grayish, developing on long, ghost-gray stems.

HEIGHT 10 to 18 inches in late spring, 32 to 38 inches in bloom.

SPREAD 14 to 16 inches in two years, 18 to 24 inches in five years.

BLOOM TIME Mid-July into late September.

GROWING CONDITIONS Average, well-drained soil in full sun; does well in drier conditions.

FIRST DATE *Perovskia atriplicifolia* 'Little Spire' 40% / *Coreopsis verticillata* 'Grandiflora' 60%

Very stylish, vertical/upright to slightly arching structure, long bloom time, and pleasant winter appearance. Cut back in mid-June to about 12 inches; this will keep the plant somewhat shorter and more upright through the season. In mid- to late March, cut 4 to 6 inches from the ground. Lives nicely on average rainfall once established; declines quickly when heavily mulched each year and watered too often.

Phlox paniculata **'Blue Paradise'** (garden phlox)

FLOWER Round, flat, ¾ inch wide, medium blue, in clusters atop the stems.

FOLIAGE Lance-shaped, ½ to ¾ inch wide, 2 to 3 inches long, developing opposite each other on the stem.

HEIGHT 10 to 18 inches in late spring, 36 to 44 inches in bloom.

SPREAD 14 to 18 inches in two years, 20 to 24 inches in five years.

BLOOM TIME Early July with moments of blue into early October.

GROWING CONDITIONS Average, moist soil, full sun to light shade; does not do well in dry conditions and extreme heat.

FIRST DATE *Phlox paniculata* 'Blue Paradise' 30% / *Molinia caerulea* subsp. *caerulea* 'Heidebraut' 70%

My main reason for choosing 'Blue Paradise' is the wonderfully long time it is in flower; it's the longest-flowering phlox I have seen. Stems are vertical; as the plant begins to flower, they arch out slightly. Water deeply during dry periods in July and August, at least three times each month. Powdery mildew, which afflicts most paniculata selections, has not been a major issue, but during hot weather, the foliage can have spider mites. You'll notice the foliage yellowing turn the leaf over, look closely, and you'll see the mites. I don't use 'Blue Paradise' in every planting, but if I know that the garden will be cared for thoughtfully and watered during dry periods, this plant gets cast. It's durable and when planted with an awareness of its needs would be a successful contributor to any garden. *Phlox paniculata* 'David', another fine selection that lives well for many years, is a good white with limited mildew problems.

LEFT The vertical blue flowers of *Perovskia atriplicifolia* **'Little Spire'** and the flower-to-seedheads of *Echinacea purpurea* **'Virgin'**.

RIGHT *Phlox paniculata* **'Blue Paradise'** enlivens all surrounding shapes and flowers, whether declining or emerging, over its long bloom season.

Polystichum acrostichoides
(Christmas fern)

FOLIAGE Dark green, glossy, narrow, 1½ to 2½ inches wide, many opposite leaflets going up the stem.

HEIGHT 14 to 18 inches by early June.

SPREAD 8 to 12 inches.

GROWING CONDITIONS Average, well-drained to moist soil, light to full shade.

FIRST DATE *Polystichum acrostichoides* 70% / *Hosta* 'Halcyon' 30% Interestingly beautiful. This fern's characteristics and durability make it valuable in diverse shade plantings. The foliage is very distinguished, suggesting many future planting combinations; it remains evergreen through the winter and starts browning in mid-April as the new fronds emerge from the soil. Lives well on average rainfall once established, as do all polystichums. Now you have found a new group of shade plants that will stimulate your artistic gardening sense.

Polystichum acrostichoides confirms the beauty of texture in the garden.

Rudbeckia subtomentosa
(sweet black-eyed Susan)

FLOWER 2-inch daisies, yellow with purplish brown cone, borne densely at the
top of the plant.

FOLIAGE Three-lobed on the lower part
of the plant, becoming oval, toothed,
slightly hairy, 2 to 3 inches long.

HEIGHT 10 to 18 inches in late spring,
54 to 72 inches in bloom.

SPREAD 16 to 20 inches in two years, 24
to 30 inches in five years.

BLOOM TIME Mid-July into early
September.

GROWING CONDITIONS Moist to average soil, full sun to light shade; does not
do well in dry soil.

FIRST DATE *Rudbeckia subtomentosa*
30% / *Calamagrostis ×acutiflora*
'Karl Foerster' 70%

Quite a contributor to the garden, with
vertical/upright, slightly arching habit,
long bloom time, and steady fall and
winter character. In early October the
foliage turns yellow-green, later changing to medium brown, all the while
keeping a strong vertical architecture.
It's a nice plant for the birds to flutter
through, finding food and shelter from
summer into winter.

LEFT The rich flowering of
Rudbeckia subtomentosa is
a cheerful addition to many
plant communities.

RIGHT *Nepeta* 'Early Bird'
in full bloom, welcoming
the vertical color of *Salvia
nemorosa* 'Wesuwe', the earliest blooming salvia.

Salvia nemorosa 'Wesuwe'
(meadow sage)

FLOWER Medium violet, tubular, hooded, in spikes.

FOLIAGE 2 to 3 inches, oblong, rough, deep green.

HEIGHT 18 to 24 inches in late spring and in bloom.

SPREAD 12 to 14 inches in two years, 14 to 16 inches in five years.

BLOOM TIME Early May into early July, reblooms without pruning late July into mid-September.

GROWING CONDITIONS Average, well-drained soil in full sun.

FIRST DATE *Salvia nemorosa* 'Wesuwe' 60% / *Nepeta* 'Early Bird' 40%

The dynamic plant offers rich, early color and a good, relaxed, vertical/mounding growth habit that knits well with many mounding plants of the same scale. If you cut it back by half in early July, it will rebloom in about three weeks; when it's cut back, water the plant deeply to encourage new growth. If not cut back, it will rebloom, albeit more slowly, through the older flowering stems. Lives well on average rainfall once established. Begins to decline with frequent irrigation two or more times per week will cause the plant to suffer. Some other good salvias are *S. nemorosa* 'Caradonna', *S. n.* 'Ostfriesland', *S.* ×*sylvestris* 'Blauhügel', and *S.* ×*sylvestris* 'Schneehügel'. Try mixing them together—the possibilities are endless. Have fun!

Salvia nemorosa 'Caradonna' strolls nicely through *Geranium sanguineum* 'Album'.

Sesleria autumnalis
(autumn moor grass)

FLOWER 3- to 4-inch spikes, at first strongly white-green, maturing to dark and finally light brown.

FOLIAGE About ⅛ inch wide, blue on upper surface, underside green, creating a light, soft blue-green effect.

HEIGHT 8 to 10 inches in late spring, 14 to 18 inches in bloom.

SPREAD 10 to 12 inches in two years, 12 to 16 inches in five years.

BLOOM TIME White spikes from early August into late September, turning brown into November.

GROWING CONDITIONS Average to slightly drier, well-drained soil in full sun to light shade.

FIRST DATE *Sesleria autumnalis* 40% / *Stachys officinalis* 'Hummelo' 60%

This useful grass has a very dense, vertical/mounding growth habit, slightly arching at the very top, and is easily interplanted with many perennials. Lives well on average rainfall once established and does not reseed. Cut back in late March above the area of new growth; it will respond poorly if cut to the ground.

TOP A real team effort *Sesleria autumnalis*, backed by the rose-purple spikes of *Stachys officinalis* 'Hummelo' and the lilac globes of *Allium angulosum* 'Summer Beauty'.

BOTTOM *Sesleria autumnalis* enhances the low mounding groups of *Geranium sanguineum*; and again, *Allium angulosum* 'Summer Beauty' chimes in amiably in the background.

In June the developing seedheads of *Sesleria caerulea* enhance the vertical shots of salvias and confident foliage of *Euphorbia polychroma* 'Bonfire'.

Sesleria caerulea
(spring moor grass)

FLOWER Small, tight, oval spikes, at first dark purple, then white-green, finally a soft tan.

FOLIAGE 1/16 to 1/4 inch wide, top surface glossy green, underside blue-gray.

HEIGHT 12 to 14 inches in late spring and in bloom.

SPREAD 8 to 10 inches in two years, 12 to 16 inches in five years.

BLOOM TIME Mid-April into late June, at which time the seedheads are soft tan.

GROWING CONDITIONS Average, well-drained soil in full sun to part shade; does well in drier conditions.

FIRST DATE *Sesleria caerulea* 60% / *Geranium sanguineum* 'Max Frei' 40%

This valuable mounding grass comes off both green and blue—a unique look that accents all its neighbors—and maintains its habit consistently through the year, into December's snowy weather. Another very good transitional plant, adaptable as far as light requirements go, it fills space well and relates one garden habitat to another. When you cut it back in March, always be sure not to cut below the growing point. That's where the new two-toned foliage immerges in spring. Find that area. As the plant ages, the growing point gets a little higher each season.

Solidago sphacelata 'Golden Fleece' (goldenrod)

FLOWER Dense, narrow, arching plumes, bright yellow, 3 to 6 inches long. The flowering stems are closely grouped, energetically spraying up and outward.

FOLIAGE Rounded, somewhat heart-shaped, toothed, dark green, 3 to 4½ inches long, developing into a layered mound.

HEIGHT 5 to 10 inches in late spring, 18 to 22 inches in bloom.

SPREAD 10 to 14 inches in two years, 18 to 24 inches in five years.

BLOOM TIME Late August into mid-October.

GROWING CONDITIONS Average, well-drained soil in full sun to light shade.

FIRST DATE *Solidago sphacelata* 'Golden Fleece' 40% / *Monarda bradburiana* 60% A plant of sturdy character and positive qualities. Its mounding growth habit accents other perennials nicely, and its beautiful spring and summer foliage is followed by a late summer and fall of bright flower color and a winter of structural beauty. Cut back in March, and then sit back and enjoy it all again. Lives well on average rainfall once established.

Spodiopogon sibiricus (graybeard grass)

FLOWER Soft grayish brown, upright, narrow yet open panicles.

FOLIAGE Medium green, ½ inch wide, 4 to 8 inches long, developing horizontally on the stems.

HEIGHT 12 to 18 inches in late spring, 36 to 42 inches in bloom.

SPREAD 10 to 18 inches in two years, 24 to 34 inches in five years.

BLOOM TIME Late July into October.

GROWING CONDITIONS Average, well-drained to moist soil, full sun to part shade.

FIRST DATE *Spodiopogon sibiricus* 40% / *Rudbeckia subtomentosa* 60%

LEFT *Solidago sphacelata* 'Golden Fleece' never fails to create quality relationships in the garden.

CENTER The slim, horizontal dashes of *Spodiopogon sibiricus*'s foliage are a visual pleasure, contrasting subtly with the more substantive foliage and verticality of many plants.

RIGHT The finely textured new growth of *Sporobolus heterolepis* spikes a mixed planting of *Geranium sanguineum*.

A beautiful grass, with great character! The flower heads are uncommonly nice; the panicles are sufficiently separated, so that the gaps between them help define their shape. And despite our tendency to think of green as a nonevent in the garden, even green can't help but be stimulating the way spodiopogon's foliage layers it up. In less light, this grass will have a looser appearance; in average soils, water deeply two or three times in both July and August to keep it looking good. Fall color is reddish yellow. When you see this grass in a container at the garden center, it will look unimpressive. Be patient. It is slow to define itself the first two years; after that, it develops its handsome mounded shape. Every four to five years, in April, you can divide this grass into fist-sized divisions, which you can then share with your local garden club. Too few are aware of this plant give people the chance to come to know and appreciate it in their own gardens.

Sporobolus heterolepis
(prairie dropseed)

FLOWER Open, airy panicles on long, arching flowering stems.
FOLIAGE Medium green, about ⅛ inch wide, developing from the plant's base with a brush-like appearance in late May into late June, then quietly arching over, creating stunning, soft mounds.
HEIGHT 6 to 9 inches in late spring, 28 to 40 inches in bloom.
SPREAD 12 to 18 inches in two years, 22 to 28 inches in five years.
BLOOM TIME Mid-August into October.
GROWING CONDITIONS Average, well-drained soil; does very nicely in dry or slightly moist conditions.
FIRST DATE *Sporobolus heterolepis* 60% / *Kalimeris incisa* 'Blue Star' 40%

This see-thru grass doesn't seem to mind anything—it's very forgiving! And no matter who views it, everyone has a nice emotional response. It's almost like a sunrise or sunset—nobody has too many complaints. Can be slow to establish; it begins to have a full look the third year. At bloom time the foliage is 14 to 16 inches tall; in late September, it begins turning yellow-green, then golden yellow. The flowering stems have the same golden tones. You can cut this grass low in March; the new growth emerges just below the soil and begins to green up in late April. In between lies a great opportunity for bulbs to fill the open spaces; after the show, in late May, let the grass cover the declining bulb foliage. When sporobolus begins to flower, it has a distinctly . . . extroverted fragrance; I was introduced to the scent as "hot buttered popcorn," so it remains appealing for me, but this is just to say one way or another, it will be noticed. 'Tara' is my own introduction, a selection I found around Bald Bluff in Wisconsin's Kettle Moraine; its foliage is shorter and more upright.

Stachys officinalis 'Hummelo'
(betony)

FLOWER 2 to 3 inches, rich purple, borne in spikes 6 to 8 inches above the foliage.
FOLIAGE 2 to 3 inches, oval, slightly crinkled, medium green, develops a layered look.
HEIGHT 14 to 18 inches in late spring, 16 to 22 inches in bloom.
SPREAD 6 to 8 inches in two years, 9 to 14 inches in five years.
BLOOM TIME Late June into early August.
GROWING CONDITIONS Average, slightly moist to well-drained soil in full sun to part shade.
FIRST DATE *Stachys officinalis* 'Hummelo' 60% / *Sporobolus heterolepis* 40%

This clump-forming plant with clean, durable foliage is an aesthetic beauty from the moment it begins to develop in mid-April. It has a vertical/mounding growth habit, and its flowering stems don't lean. In mid-August the flower spikes start to turn an attractive dark brown, a look which lasts until the plant is cut back in March. *Stachys officinalis* 'Rosea' and *S. o.* 'Cotton Candy' are also nice; mix two or three of these into a group of four to 10 'Hummelo'. The color tones are too good!

LEFT *Stachys officinalis* 'Hummelo' (and a bit of *S. o.* 'Rosea'), fronting *Coreopsis verticillata* 'Grandiflora'.

RIGHT Lace and leather *Thalictrum dioicum* with *Asarum canadense* in the foreground.

Thalictrum dioicum
(early meadow rue)

FLOWER Small, greenish white, in drooping clusters, borne above the developing foliage.
FOLIAGE Rounded, slightly toothed, ½ inch in diameter, gray-green, compound, grouped openly on narrow, thin stems, maturing into a densely layered mound.
HEIGHT 18 to 24 inches in late spring and in bloom.
SPREAD 10 to 14 inches in two years, 16 to 20 inches in five years.
BLOOM TIME Late April into mid-May.
GROWING CONDITIONS Average, well-drained soil in light shade to part shade.
FIRST DATE *Thalictrum dioicum* 30% / *Carex shortiana* 70%

This excellent, lacy, fine-textured, structural species adds nothing but beauty to the shade garden, but it will reseed. The seedlings are unmistakable you can leave them to blend into your existing planting or relocate them to other garden areas. This is a wonderful plant that we all need to get to know. It's long-lived, easy to enjoy, and lives well on average rainfall. Appreciates leaf mulch every two to three years.

Tulipa 'Spring Green'
(viridiflora tulip)

FLOWER Classic tulip, pale yellow-white with streaks of lime-green.

FOLIAGE Upright, slightly arching, 1 inch wide, 8 to 10 inches high.

HEIGHT 14 to 16 inches in bloom.

BLOOM TIME May.

GROWING CONDITIONS Average, well-drained soil, full sun to part shade.

This early bulb offers a flower color that is easy to mix within many perennial plant communities. Use in groups of four to nine, placing the bulbs about 3 inches from each other. Cut the flowering stems off into the foliage when they are through. Another viridiflora tulip, *Tulipa* 'Golden Artist', has a golden-yellow flower streaked with green.

Vernonia lettermannii 'Iron Butterfly' (ironweed)

FLOWER Clusters of small, violet-purple florets, held atop the plant.

FOLIAGE Very narrow, dark green, 2½ to 4 inches long, clustered densely along stems, which themselves develop closely.

HEIGHT 2 to 4 inches in late May, 32 to 38 inches in bloom.

SPREAD 9 to 14 inches in two years, 20 to 26 inches in five years.

BLOOM TIME September into October.

GROWING CONDITIONS Average, well-drained soil in full sun; does well in drier conditions.

FIRST DATE *Vernonia lettermannii* 'Iron Butterfly' 30% / *Sporobolus heterolepis* 70%

The dark, superbly fine-textured foliage, the rich purple flowers in late summer—what *can't* you do with this plant? For three years now, I have been using it to accent many varied styles of plantings. During the hot, dry summer of 2012 I did water during July and August; the year before it lived well with our average rainfall. This perennial adds value to any garden!

LEFT *Tulipa* 'Spring Green', here mixed with complementary grape hyacinths.

RIGHT Including the painterly texture and beautifully dark colors of *Vernonia lettermannii* 'Iron Butterfly' is an easy way to move your garden in the "art" direction.

Chapter 6

The Garden Plans

The garden plans are the building blocks of the Know Maintenance system. They are designed to get you off to a solid beginning. Each plan is a plant community of young plants, placed to live well growing closely together, their health and beauty shared with you. And each has been designed in a simple way, according to basic principles. I believe you should plant only up to your capabilities; then, as you and the plants build relationships with each other over time, a satisfying awareness develops within you. Your garden is healthy and, what's more, you understand why. You have a heightened sense of ecology. The weather, the soil, the light—all are associated with the well-being of your plants. You'll get a clear view of what is ahead for you and garden. And with all your five senses fired by the beauty springing up around you, and with maintenance more or less off your "to do" list, you are free to discover the joy of gardening, which is the simplest principle of all.

The plans aren't really a new development. But that isn't important—newness in itself isn't a virtue. What matters is that the plants in them have been chosen and positioned to live well together with respect to their common needs and individual lifestyles. Beginning with such a plan ensures that your garden gets off to a good start. Evaluate, use intuition, and carry out knowledge-based actions to introduce new elements as you understand their value and role in the garden.

It's simple: each plant around the other—from leaves to stems to flowers—paints an Impressionistic moment. The garden plans don't demand that one plant do all the entertaining. Rather, many plants freely and comfortably contribute.

The garden plans aren't intended to be absolutely static—they're meant to evolve, with you, over time. And this evolution can always be at your own pace. Some of the changes may result from your observation of how the plants behave, and when (or whether) you choose to intervene. Other changes may stem from your artistic passion to add, expand, or remove various elements of the planting. You're always in charge.

Let's look at what a garden plan consists of:

- Each plan is a rectangle, 10 feet by 14 feet, divided into 1-foot grids and showing the placement of every plant and bulb. The accompanying plant lists restate the total quantity of every perennial called for in each plan, as well as the number of bulbs (per area).
- The plans are presented in pairs and grouped into 30 themes (21 for sun and nine for shade), loosely inspired by either a successful public planting or garden, or by the shifts of tones, color, and pattern in an Impressionist painting. Looking at great works of art is always enlightening: the depth of emotion that you see on the canvas—and within each artist—will enrich how you see and interact with your own garden canvas.
- Each paired set of garden plans has descriptive remarks and notes on maintenance. These are meant to provide you with some guidance about how the planting will develop from its earliest stages and to help you anticipate what care will be needed in the future. Take your own notes about plant growth, blooming dates, and especially about any conditions that affect the health and appearance of the garden. If you do this over the course of the growing season, and from year to year, you will become much closer to your garden and have a clearer perspective on what you need to do and when you need to do it.
- When you're deciding which plan you'd like to begin with, always relate your selection to the site you've chosen. Your selection should be in tune aesthetically with the surrounding features. Above all, you'll need to be sure there is sufficient light and that the site has access to water. Consider, too, if it is large enough to allow you to add more plantings later (if you think you might want to).
- The bottom of each plan represents the front of the garden. However, there's no reason why some grids

can't be flipped—it depends on the site and on the specific plants involved. You can be a little edgy—remember, you're not doing this to please others.

- You can connect the paired plans, or repeat one with itself then add the other. You can mix plans from different themes, but you should understand their characteristics before you combine them. Don't act too quickly. Again, the idea is to know what you're getting into. The possible combinations are numerous.
- Each plan should take an average of three to four and a half hours of work per season. If you cut the plants back with a mulching mower, it will be even less. That assumes, of course, that you're diligent about care and maintenance. If you miss some gardening days, the amount of time you need to spend may double—especially if you don't take care of weeding in May!

Take your time to become familiar with the plans. Look at the plants in each one, read a little about them in the previous chapter, then read a little more. Patience is the most important quality of the good gardener and the most important aspect of gardening to pass along to others. Observe the placement of the plants together, the percentages of each used, and what their closest neighbors are. It's all about relationships!

This isn't an idle exercise: the more familiar you are with the plants, the better you'll be able to visualize the plan. One of the most enjoyable moments in my life occurred in 2001, when I met Dutch designer Piet Oudolf at Northwind. Oudolf's team had just won the design competition for the Lurie Garden in Chicago's Millennium Park, and he needed to partner with a local nursery to source the plants. When he arrived, we toured the nursery; then he rolled out his plan on an old picnic table. I focused on the plant patterns and plant names, and suddenly I could see the whole garden lift off the paper. Piet's writing disappeared and the garden became real; I could clearly see how beautifully original it would be, unlike anything ever planted in the Midwest. I saw the textures, colors, heights, the blending of plant groups. The garden came to life because I had come to know these plants over the years at Northwind Perennial Farm. Moments like this can be yours too, in time. Now, on to the garden plans!

Walk this way: the garden plans are a path to a new style of gardening. And each autumn, the earth tones and strong textures of the plants in them return, by various routes, to what makes something beautiful: simplicity.

Swarthmore College Campus

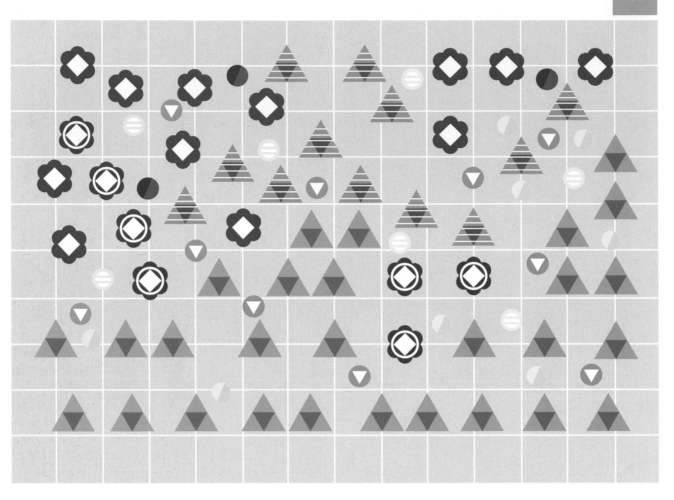

MAINTENANCE NOTES The salvia could be trimmed back by half in mid-July, resulting in strong rebloom in mid-August, or you can allow the new flowers to develop through the old flowering stems—makes for a very nice look, full of contrast. Observe the vernonia; you may need to add some to balance the grass/echinacea percentages. This is an easy planting to cut back and clean up in mid-March. Leave all the clippings around the plants—the plants will live healthily in their own debris.

REMARKS Swarthmore's campus, just outside Philadelphia, has a thoughtful calmness and serenity that blends old and new. This planting celebrates and echoes that special place with simple colors and contrasting textures.

Sesleria caerulea **28**

Stachys officinalis '*Hummelo*' **12**

Sporobolus heterolepis **12**

Salvia nemorosa '*Ostfriesland*' **7**

EARLY BULBS

Chionodoxa forbesii **5–6 per area**

Narcissus '*Lemon Drops*' **4–6 per area**

Allium moly **4–5 per area**

Allium atropurpureum **1–2 per area**

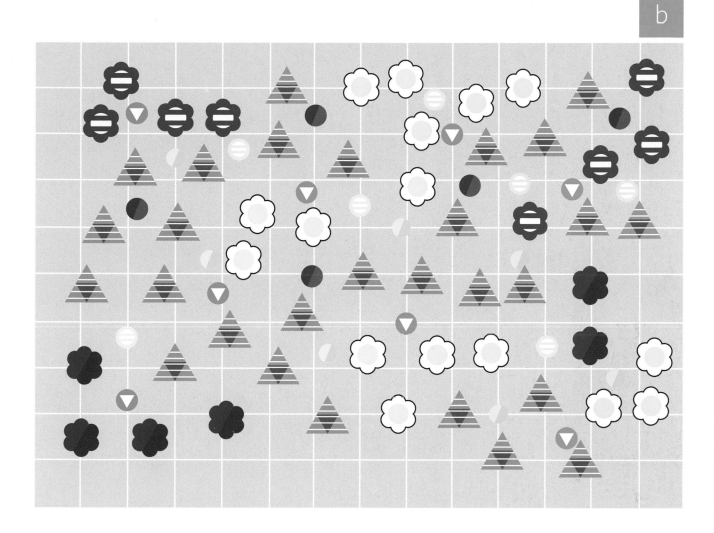

Sporobolus heterolepis **28**	**EARLY BULBS**
Echinacea purpurea 'Virgin' **16**	Chionodoxa forbesii **5–6 per area**
Vernonia lettermannii 'Iron Butterfly' **8**	Narcissus 'Lemon Drops' **4–6 per area**
Geranium 'Orion' **6**	Allium moly **4–5 per area**
	Allium atropurpureum **2 per area**

Great Dixter

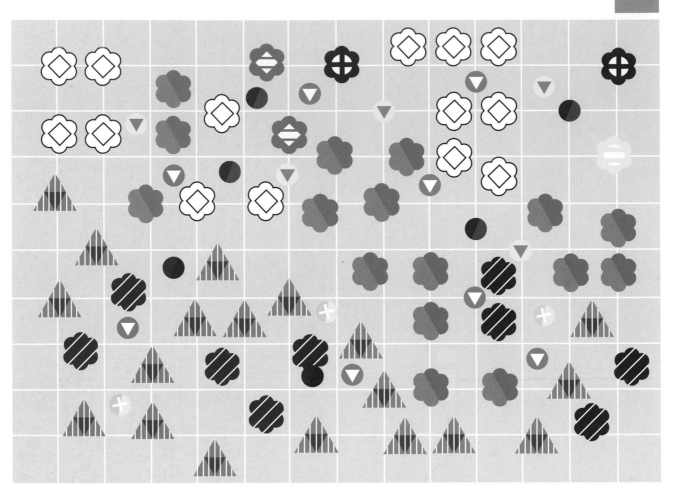

MAINTENANCE NOTES It's all about keeping things in balance. As the seasons go by, the changes keep up or add to the energy of the garden. All plantings are dynamic, and at England's Great Dixter the level of dynamism is high. Review the chapter on care and maintenance for helpful reminders.

REMARKS A fresh and exciting planting. The vivid violet spikes of the salvia highlight the warm copper-red foliage of the euphorbia; the nepeta adds soft pink to the rich purple spikes of the stachys. All await the mounded purplish pink flowers of the eupatorium.

Sesleria autumnalis **19**

Allium angulosum 'Summer Beauty' **16**

Calamintha nepeta **14**

Euphorbia polychroma 'Bonfire' **9**

Eupatorium dubium 'Baby Joe' **2**

Nepeta subsessilis Sweet Dreams' **2**

Coreopsis verticillata 'Grandiflora' **1**

EARLY BULBS

Chionodoxa forbesii **5–6 per area**

Allium flavum **4–5 per area**

Tulipa 'Golden Artist' **3–5 per area**

Allium atropurpureum **2 per area**

Allium cristophii **1–2 per area**

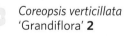

EARLY BULBS

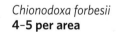

Sesleria autumnalis **33**	*Allium flavum* **4–5 per area**
Stachys officinalis 'Hummelo' **11**	*Chionodoxa forbesii* **4–5 per area**
Salvia nemorosa 'Wesuwe' **6**	*Tulipa* 'Golden Artist' **3–5 per area**
Euphorbia polychroma 'Bonfire' **5**	*Allium atropurpureum* **2 per area**
Spodiopogon sibiricus **3**	*Allium cristophii* **1–2 per area**
Coreopsis verticillata 'Grandiflora' **2**	
Eupatorium dubium 'Baby Joe' **2**	
Nepeta subsessilis 'Sweet Dreams' **2**	

The High Line

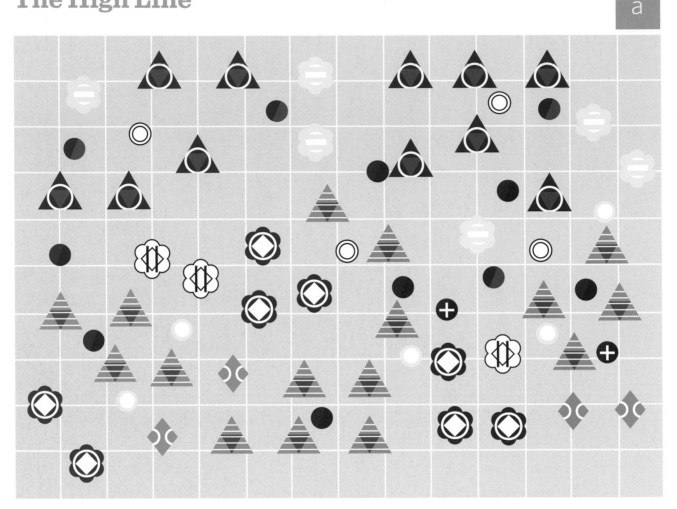

MAINTENANCE NOTES As this planting matures, maintain balance by thinning or dividing. Watch the carex, coreopsis, and panicum. Nothing will happen immediately—it's later that we become forgetful. Through the season, write down your garden thoughts and plan time to carry them out.

REMARKS New York City's High Line planting, designed by Piet Oudolf, taught gardeners about the beauty of ornamental grasses. There and in this garden, which captures the essence of that elevated park, the grasses escort you through the planting, enhancing its changeful moment-by-moment patterns.

Sporobolus heterolepis **16**

Panicum virgatum 'Heiliger Hain' or *P. v.* 'Ruby Ribbons' **11**

Salvia nemorosa 'Ostfriesland' **8**

Coreopsis verticillata 'Grandiflora' **6**

Carex flacca **4**

Salvia ×sylvestris 'Schneehügel' **3**

EARLY BULBS

 Allium carinatum subsp. *pulchellum* **4–5 per area**

Narcissus 'Quail' **3–5 per area**

Narcissus 'Thalia' **3–5 per area**

Allium atropurpureum **2 per area**

Allium cristophii **1–2 per area**

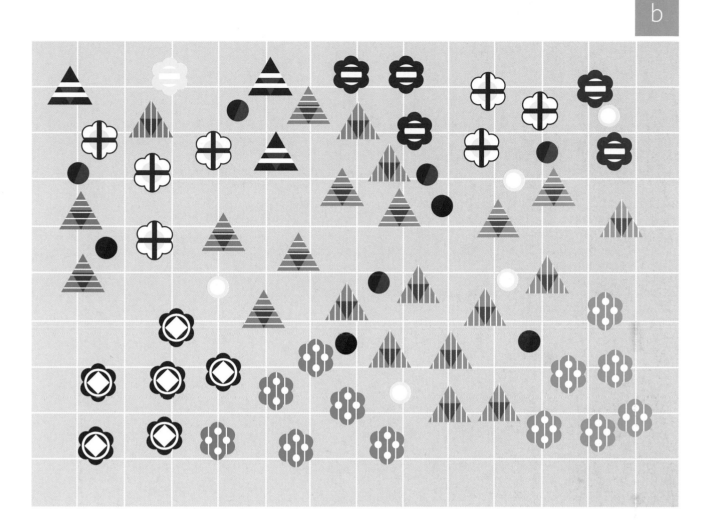

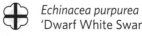

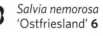

Amsonia 'Blue Ice' **12**

Sporobolus
heterolepis **10**

Sesleria autumnalis **12**

Echinacea purpurea
'Dwarf White Swan' **7**

Salvia nemorosa
'Ostfriesland' **6**

Vernonia lettermannii
'Iron Butterfly' **5**

Panicum virgatum
'Heiliger Hain' **3**

Coreopsis verticillata
'Grandiflora' **1**

EARLY BULBS

Narcissus 'Quail'
3–5 per area

Allium atropurpureum
2 per area

Allium cristophii
1–2 per area

Essence of Piet Oudolf

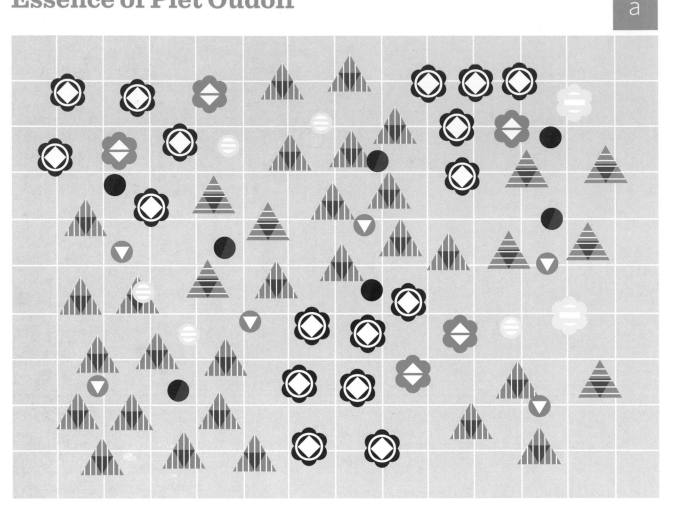

MAINTENANCE NOTES This sturdy group has some moments when you could prune to promote rebloom. Both salvias could be trimmed back by half in mid-July, resulting in strong rebloom in mid-August. You could also allow new flowers to develop through the old flowering stems, for a more spirited look. See what look fits your style. In March, don't cut the sesleria down below the growing point; look carefully and you'll see where the new foliage develops from the stems at the base of the plant.

REMARKS Many textures contribute to the mood of this pair of plans. Spikes of purple and blue salvias set off the mounds of the sesleria and the soft, medium green of the coreopsis. Piet Oudolf enjoys what he calls "the playfulness of plants"—the constant, interactive movement of foliage, stems, flowers, and seedheads, like children in a schoolyard.

Sesleria autumnalis **26**

Salvia nemorosa 'Ostfriesland' **17**

Sporobolus heterolepis **8**

Salvia ×sylvestris 'Blauhügel' **5**

Coreopsis verticillata 'Grandiflora' **2**

EARLY BULBS

Chionodoxa forbesii **5–6 per area**

Narcissus 'Lemon Drops' **4–6 per area**

Allium atropurpureum **1–2 per area**

Allium cristophii **1–2 per area**

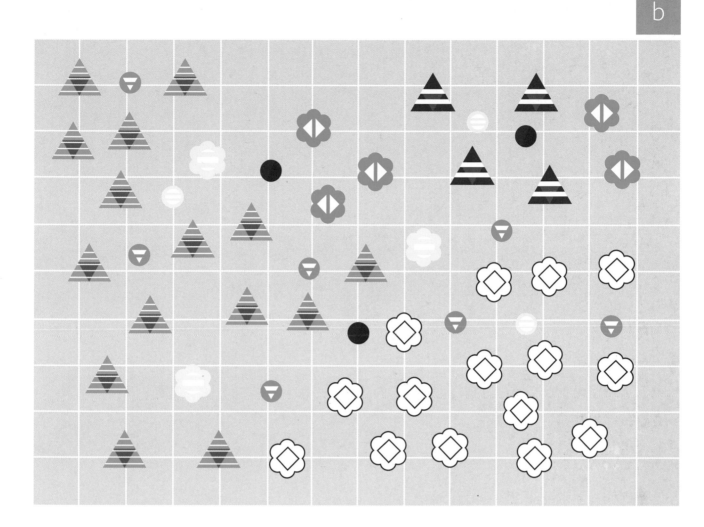

 Calamintha nepeta **15**

 Sporobolus heterolepis **15**

 Agastache 'Blue Fortune' **5**

▲ *Panicum virgatum* 'Heiliger Hain' **4**

Coreopsis verticillata 'Grandiflora' **3**

EARLY BULBS

Narcissus 'Lemon Drops' **4–6 per area**

Camassia quamash **4–5 per area**

● *Allium cristophii* **1–2 per area**

Bonnard, *Earthly Paradise*

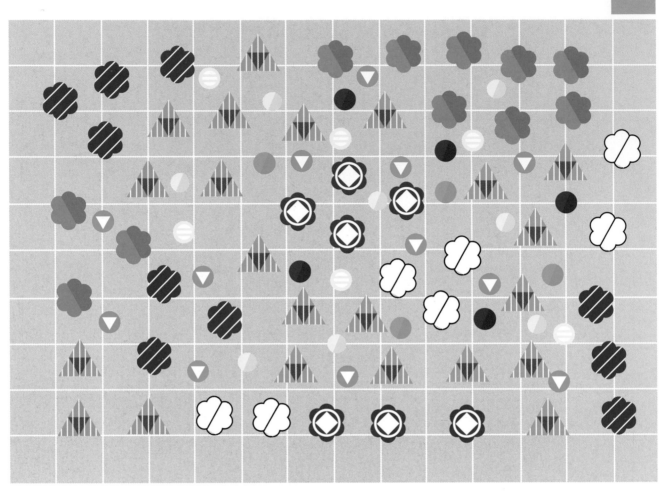

MAINTENANCE NOTES The salvia could be trimmed back by half in mid-July, resulting in strong rebloom in mid-August, or just let the plants rebloom through their old flowering stems—it's a nice look. The flowering stems of the alliums turn red-yellow in fall—don't cut them back. In March, don't cut the sesleria down below the growing point; look carefully and you'll see where the new foliage develops from the stems at the base of the plant.

REMARKS I designed this garden for the Art Institute of Chicago. In it, the stachys remains strongly vertical until it is cut back in March. The kalimeris will reseed modestly; be sure to remove the seedlings—they will grow taller and more open and reseed at a high rate.

Sesleria autumnalis **22**

Allium angulosum 'Summer Beauty' **11**

Euphorbia polychroma 'Bonfire' **10**

Geranium sanguineum 'Album' **7**

Salvia nemorosa 'Ostfriesland' **7**

EARLY BULBS

Allium caeruleum **5–6 per area**

Chionodoxa forbesii **5–6 per area**

Narcissus 'Lemon Drops' **4–6 per area**

Allium moly **4–5 per area**

Allium cristophii **1–2 per area**

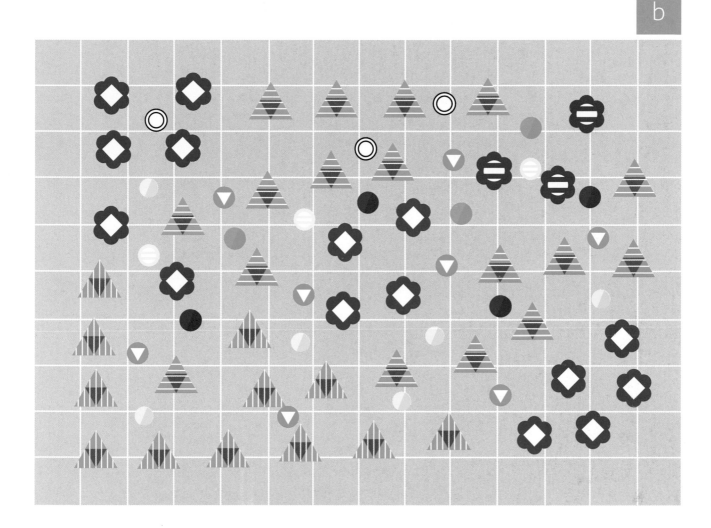

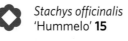

Sporobolus heterolepis **17**

Stachys officinalis
'Hummelo' **15**

Sesleria autumnalis **12**

Kalimeris incisa
'Blue Star' **3**

EARLY BULBS

Chionodoxa forbesii
5–6 per area

Narcissus
'Lemon Drops'
4–6 per area

Allium moly
4–5 per area

Narcissus 'Thalia'
4–5 per area

Allium cristophii
1–2 per area

Bonnard, *Earthly Paradise*, contd.

a

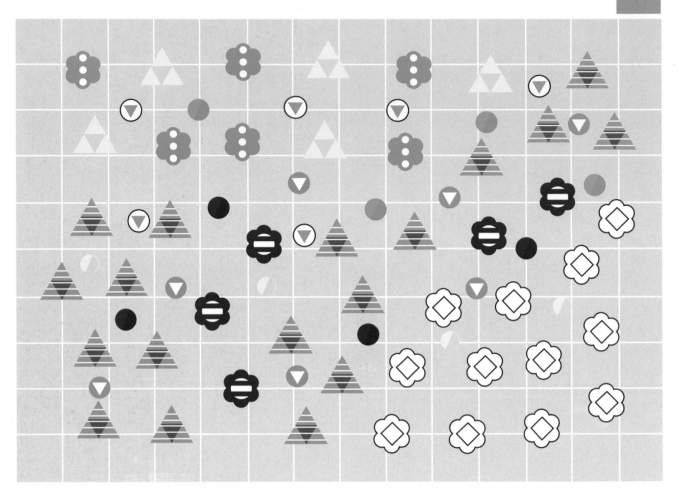

MAINTENANCE NOTES The phlox will benefit from deep waterings during dry periods in July and August, at least three times each month. Make certain the water gets to the root zone of the plants. Remove the old flower stems from the tulips after blooming is finished. Keep an eye on the kalimeris reseeding; remember, the seedlings are much bigger than 'Blue Star'.

REMARKS This planting is bound together by the fluid motion of the grasses. They enclose the mounding white of the echinacea and support and enhance the dark, rich foliage and purple flowers of the alliums and the lavender clouds of limonium.

Sporobolus heterolepis **18**

Calamintha nepeta **12**

Phlox paniculata 'Blue Paradise' **6**

Calamagrostis ×*acutiflora* 'Karl Foerster' **5**

Kalimeris incisa 'Blue Star' **5**

EARLY BULBS

Allium caeruleum **5–6 per area**

Chionodoxa forbesii **5–6 per area**

Allium moly **4–5 per area**

Tulipa 'Spring Green' **3–5 per area**

Allium cristophii **1–2 per area**

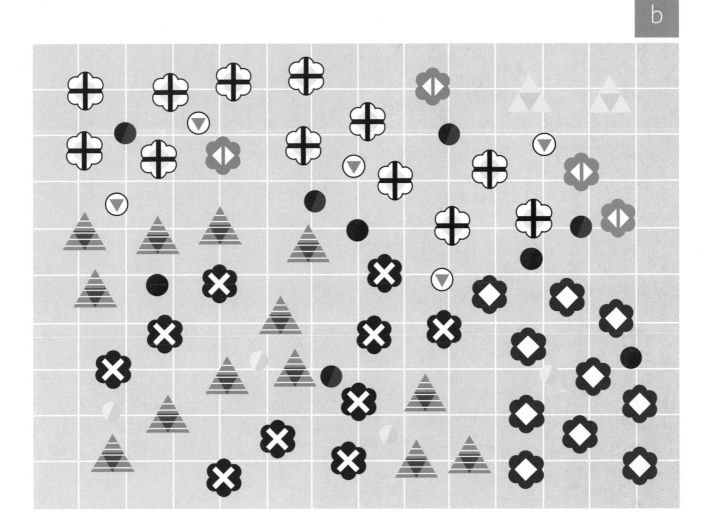

	Sporobolus heterolepis **13**	**EARLY BULBS**	
	Echinacea purpurea 'Dwarf White Swan' **12**		*Allium moly* **4–5 per area**
	Limonium latifolium **10**		*Tulipa* 'Spring Green' **3–5 per area**
	Stachys officinalis 'Hummelo' **10**		*Allium atropurpureum* **2 per area**
	Agastache 'Blue Fortune' **4**		*Allium cristophii* **1–2 per area**
	Calamagrostis ×*acutiflora* 'Karl Foerster' **2**		

Art Deco

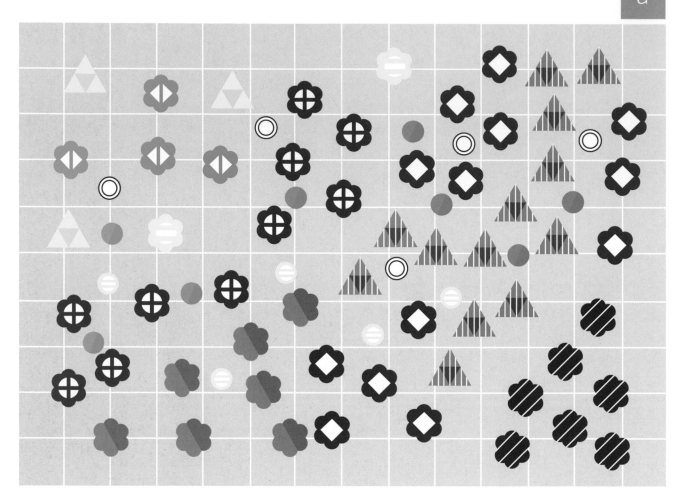

MAINTENANCE NOTES The coreopsis spreads by rhizomes; plants maintain a tight habit, but they do expand. In four to five years you may need to thin them to maintain the balance with the echinacea.

REMARKS The vertical lavender-blue spikes of the agastache contrast with the mounding, golden yellow coreopsis. The excitement continues as the blue-green mound of the baptisia softens the rich purple spikes of the stachys.

Stachys officinalis 'Hummelo' **13**

Sesleria autumnalis **13**

Echinacea 'Pixie Meadowbrite' **10**

Allium angulosum 'Summer Beauty' **7**

Euphorbia polychroma 'Bonfire' **7**

Agastache 'Blue Fortune' **4**

Calamagrostis ×acutiflora 'Karl Foerster' **3**

Coreopsis verticillata 'Grandiflora' **2**

EARLY BULBS

Allium caeruleum **5–7 per area**

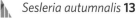

Narcissus 'Lemon Drops' **4–6 per area**

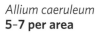
Narcissus 'Thalia' **4–6 per area**

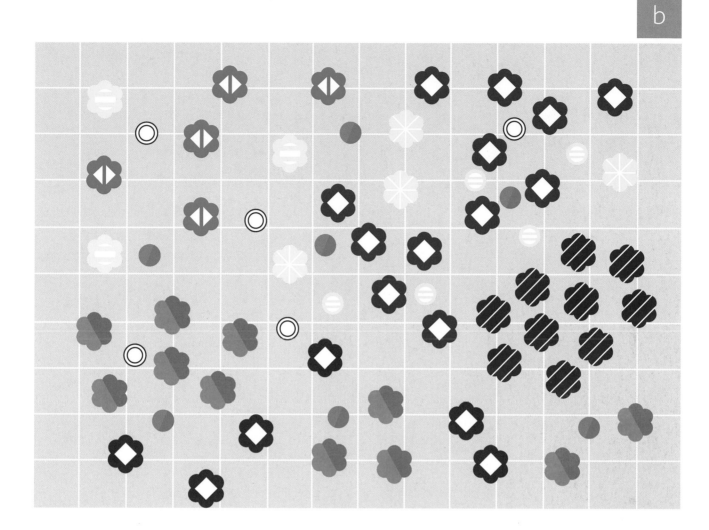

Stachys officinalis 'Hummelo' **12**

Allium angulosum 'Summer Beauty' **11**

Euphorbia polychroma 'Bonfire' **10**

Nepeta 'Early Bird' **6**

Agastache 'Blue Fortune' **5**

Baptisia sphaerocarpa 4

Coreopsis verticillata 'Grandiflora' **3**

EARLY BULBS

Allium caeruleum **5–7 per area**

Narcissus 'Lemon Drops' **4–6 per area**

Narcissus 'Thalia' **4–6 per area**

van Gogh, *Poet's Garden*

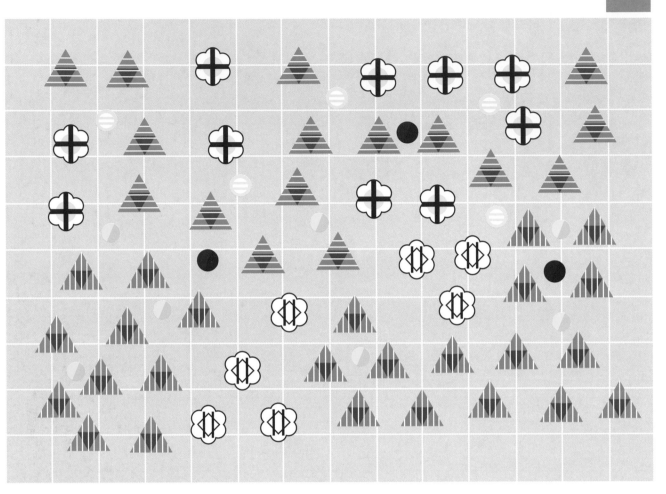

MAINTENANCE NOTES The salvia could be trimmed back by half in mid-July, resulting in strong rebloom in mid-August, or you can let plants rebloom through the old flowering stems. The echinacea will reseed lightly; you can decide how they will live within the planting, or you may choose to move them to another location. This is another grouping of plants that can be cut back in March; the debris can then be distributed around the plants. Remove the old flower stems of the tulips as soon as they are done flowering.

REMARKS The cloud-like white flowers of the parthenium highlight the fine-textured mounds of the golden yellow coreopsis; they all settle into the soft green of the sporobolus. It takes a bit to get there, but the eventual look is of a fantastically intricate tapestry.

Sesleria autumnalis **25**

Sporobolus heterolepis **16**

Echinacea purpurea 'Dwarf White Swan' **10**

Salvia ×*sylvestris* 'Schneehügel' **7**

EARLY BULBS

Narcissus 'Lemon Drops' **5–6 per area**

Allium moly **4–5 per area**

Allium cristophii **1–2 per area**

Sporobolus heterolepis **36**

Echinacea purpurea 'Dwarf White Swan' **10**

Parthenium integrifolium **5**

Solidago sphacelata 'Golden Fleece' **4**

Coreopsis verticillata 'Grandiflora' **2**

EARLY BULBS

Narcissus 'Lemon Drops' **5–6 per area**

Allium moly **4–5 per area**

Tulipa 'Golden Artist' **4–5 per area**

Allium cristophii **1–2 per area**

Seurat, *The Rue St. Vincent*

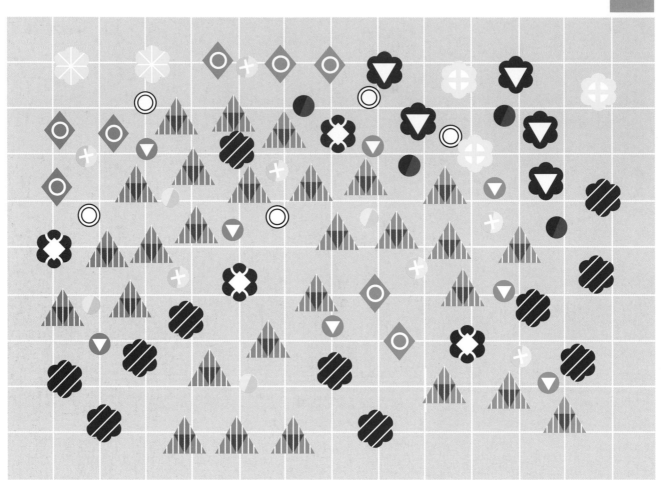

MAINTENANCE NOTES The most concentrated spell of work, as in most of the planting grids, is cutting back the plants in mid-March. Be sure to leave all the debris around the plants—it's not messy, it's healthy! Watch the achillea and how it relates to neighboring plants; it may need thinning or division in four years.

REMARKS The bright yellow baptisia and achillea are the focus in this pattern of plants. The coppery red foliage of the euphorbia contrasts with the other green foliage until late July, when the brilliant red of the daylily creates an intense moment.

Sesleria autumnalis **28**

Euphorbia polychroma 'Bonfire' **10**

Carex swanii or *Sporobolus heterolepis* **8**

Hemerocallis 'Chicago Apache' **5**

Salvia nemorosa 'Wesuwe' **4**

Achillea 'Hella Glashoff' or *A.* 'Coronation Gold' **3**

Baptisia sphaerocarpa **2**

EARLY BULBS

Chionodoxa forbesii **5–6 per area**

Allium moly **4–5 per area**

Narcissus 'Thalia' **4–5 per area**

Allium flavum **3–4 per area**

Allium atropurpureum **2 per area**

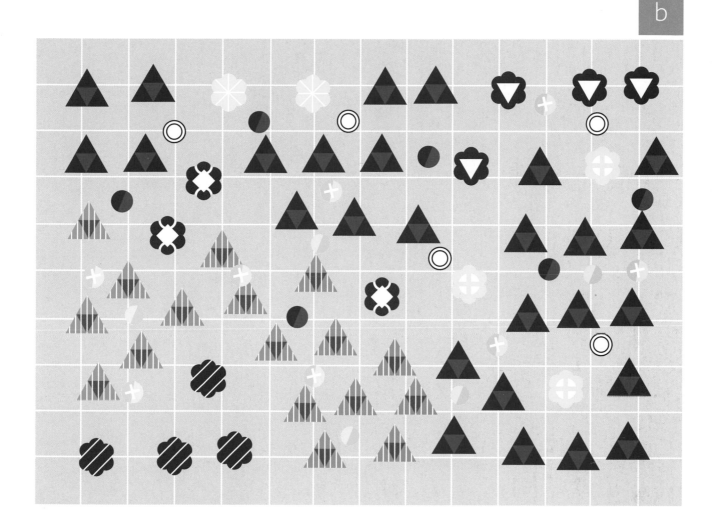

 Molinia caerulea subsp. caerulea 'Moorhexe' **27**

 Sesleria autumnalis **17**

Euphorbia polychroma 'Bonfire' **4**

 Hemerocallis 'Chicago Apache' **4**

Achillea 'Hella Glashoff' or A. 'Coronation Gold' **3**

Baptisia sphaerocarpa **2**

Salvia nemorosa 'Wesuwe' **3**

EARLY BULBS

Allium moly **4–5 per area**

Narcissus 'Thalia' **4–5 per area**

Allium flavum **3–4 per area**

Allium atropurpureum **2 per area**

Cézanne, *The Forest Clearing*

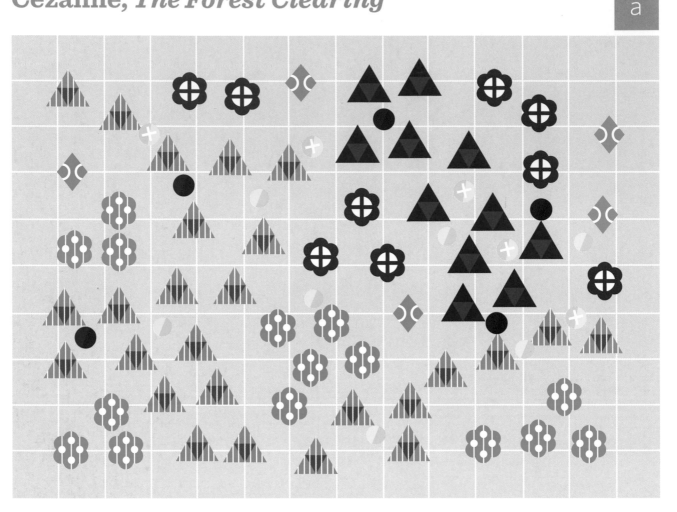

MAINTENANCE NOTES Don't be put off by the number of plants called for or the tight spacing indicated plants with vertical growth habits can be sited very close together. In March, when you cut the garden back, do not cut the sesleria below its growing point, or it will weaken or even kill the plant.

REMARKS The molinia has vertical see-thru flowering stems, slightly screening the soft pink flowers of the echinacea and creating visual layering. The sesleria and carex grow together, blending tones of green and blue.

Sesleria autumnalis **26**

Amsonia 'Blue Ice' **15**

Molinia caerulea subsp. *caerulea* 'Moorhexe' **11**

Echinacea 'Pixie Meadowbrite' **9**

Carex flacca **5**

EARLY BULBS

Allium moly **4–5 per area**

Allium flavum **3–4 per area**

Allium cristophii **1–2 per area**

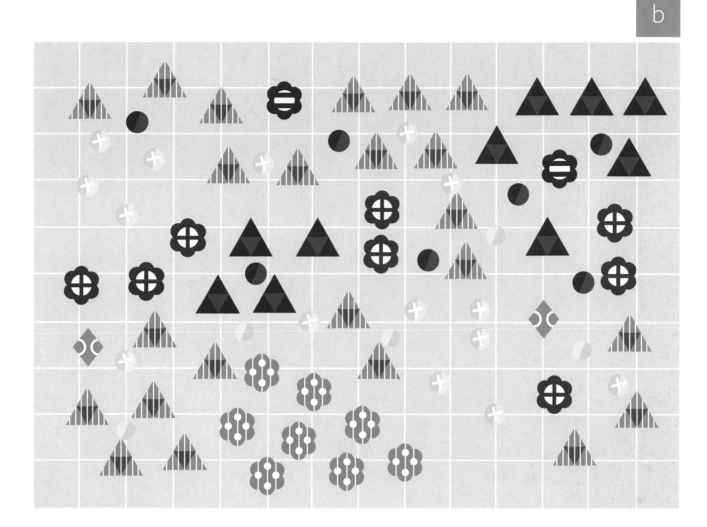

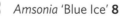
Sesleria autumnalis **30**

Molinia caerulea subsp. caerulea 'Moorhexe' **10**

Amsonia 'Blue Ice' **8**

Echinacea 'Pixie Meadowbrite' **8**

Carex flacca **2**

Kalimeris incisa 'Blue Star' **2**

EARLY BULBS

Allium moly
4–5 per area

Allium flavum
3–4 per area

Allium atropurpureum
2 per area

Renoir, *The Gust of Wind*

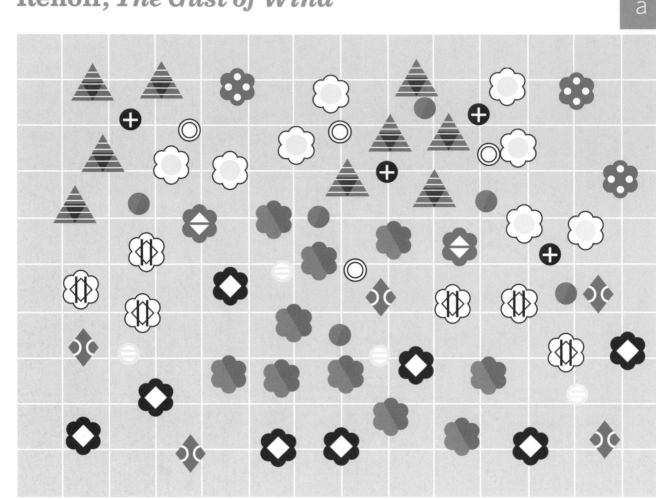

MAINTENANCE NOTES As they mature seasonally, the amsonia and carex will take up more space. Watch them closely to see whether they're crowding the other plants. If so, move some plants away from the amsonia; in the case of the carex, divide it if necessary. To fill the void in early spring, use bulbs. Remember healthy intimacy is a major aspect of a garden's beauty.

REMARKS The soft blue and clear white of the combined salvias mixes well with the textural variety of the sporobolus and echinacea foliage, later highlighted by the large white flowers of the echinacea in July and August. It is a season of blue and white.

Allium angulosum 'Summer Beauty' **10**

Sporobolus heterolepis **9**

Echinacea purpurea 'Virgin' **8**

Nepeta 'Early Bird' **8**

Salvia ×*sylvestris* 'Schneehügel' **6**

Carex flacca **5**

Amsonia tabernaemontana var. *salicifolia* **3**

Salvia ×*sylvestris* 'Blauhügel' **2**

EARLY BULBS

Allium caeruleum **4–5 per area**

Narcissus 'Lemon Drops' **4–5 per area**

Narcissus 'Thalia' **4–5 per area**

Allium carinatum subsp. *pulchellum* **3–4 per area**

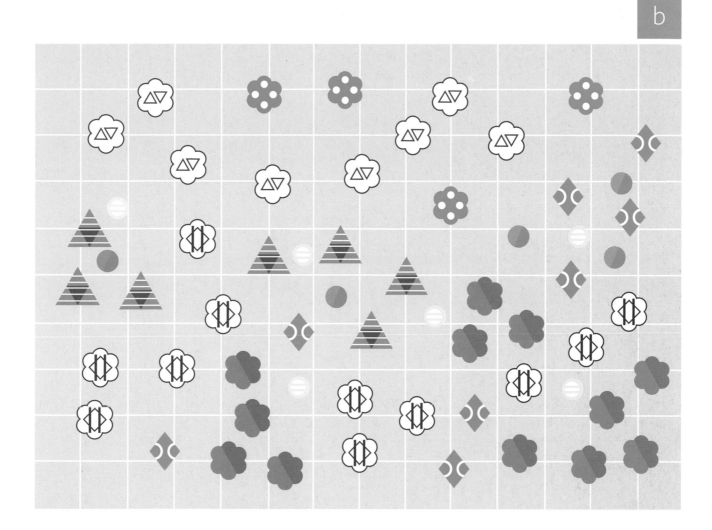

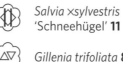 Allium angulosum
'Summer Beauty' **12**

Salvia ×sylvestris
'Schneehügel' **11**

Gillenia trifoliata **8**

Carex flacca **8**

Sporobolus heterolepis **7**

Amsonia tabernaemontana
var. salicifolia **4**

EARLY BULBS

Allium caeruleum
4–5 per area

Narcissus
'Lemon Drops'
4–5 per area

Monet, *The Artist's Garden at Vétheuil*

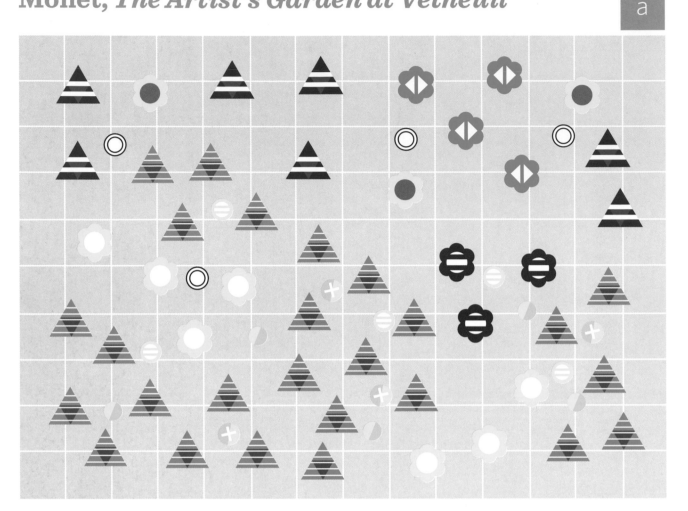

MAINTENANCE NOTES As the planting matures, keep evaluating the relationships among its members. Dividing a few plants at the three- to five-year mark could be beneficial to maintain a balanced appearance in the garden. If the rudbeckia gets too big, you can root prune it in spring just as new growth is emerging, push a tile spade through the roots at a 30-degree angle on all four sides; that should shorten the plant's development that season.

REMARKS The golden yellow rudbeckia rises above and contrasts with the soft blue kalimeris, and makes a playful companion for the vertical lavender-blue agastache. All rest within the gentle, fine-textured foliage of the sporobolus.

Sporobolus heterolepis **26**

Coreopsis palmata **7**

Panicum virgatum 'Heiliger Hain' or *P. v.* 'Ruby Ribbons' **7**

Agastache 'Blue Fortune' **4**

Rudbeckia subtomentosa **3**

Kalimeris incisa 'Blue Star' **3**

EARLY BULBS

Narcissus 'Lemon Drops' **4–6 per area**

Narcissus 'Thalia' **4–6 per area**

Allium moly **4–5 per area**

Allium flavum **3–4 per area**

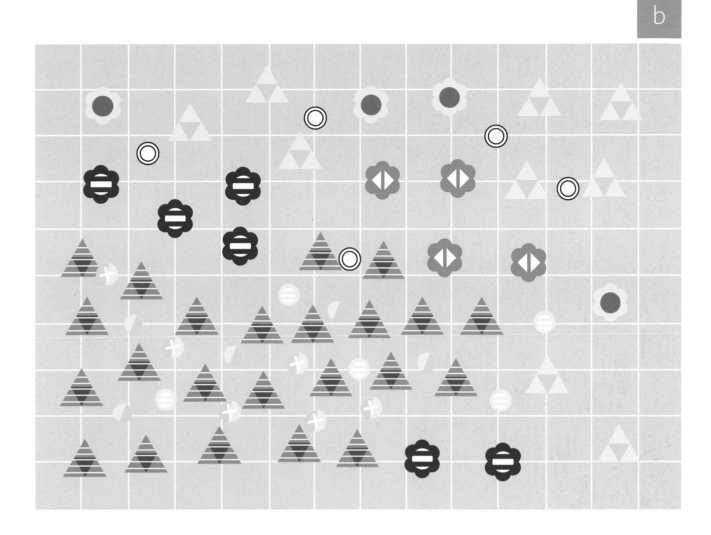

Sporobolus heterolepis **23**

Calamagrostis ×acutiflora 'Karl Foerster' **9**

Kalimeris incisa ' Blue Star' **6**

Agastache 'Blue Fortune' **4**

Rudbeckia subtomentosa **4**

EARLY BULBS

Narcissus 'Lemon Drops' **4–6 per area**

Narcissus 'Thalia' **4–6 per area**

Allium flavum **4–5 per area**

Allium moly **4–5 per area**

Monet, *Sunset on the Sea, off Pourville*

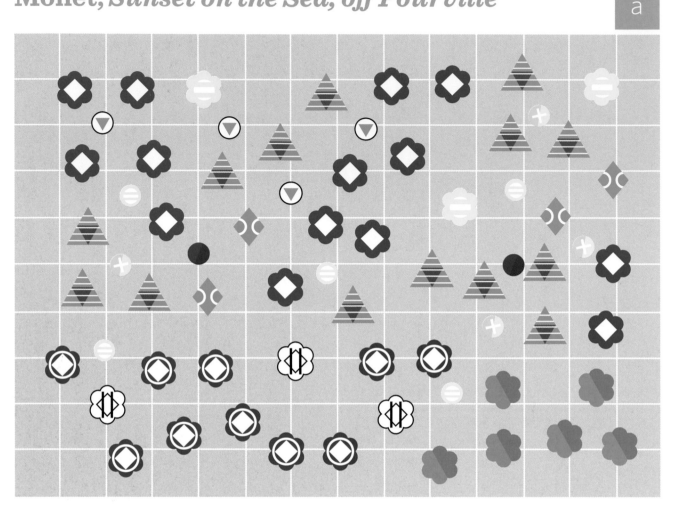

MAINTENANCE NOTES The salvias could be trimmed back by half in mid-July, resulting in strong rebloom in mid-August, or you can let plants rebloom through the old flowering stems. In mid-March, cut everything back and leave the debris in the garden around the plants. If you like, cut the stems and leaves into smaller pieces.

REMARKS Garden balance is always important. You may find spots to add more accents of salvias. Simply divide what you have and make more. Your plants will live well in this gentle meadow!

Sporobolus heterolepis **14**

Stachys officinalis 'Hummelo' **14**

Salvia nemorosa 'Ostfriesland' **10**

Allium angulosum 'Summer Beauty' **6**

Carex flacca **4**

Coreopsis verticillata 'Grandiflora' **3**

Salvia ×sylvestris 'Schneehügel' **3**

EARLY BULBS

Narcissus 'Lemon Drops' **5–6 per area**

Allium flavum **4–5 per area**

Tulipa 'Spring Green' **3–5 per area**

Allium cristophii **1–2 per area**

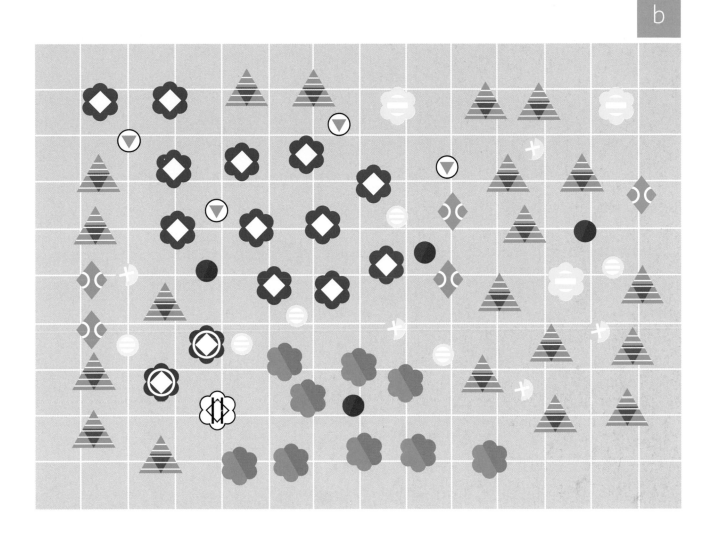

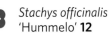

Sporobolus
heterolepis **17**

Stachys officinalis
'Hummelo' **12**

Allium angulosum
'Summer Beauty' **9**

Carex flacca **5**

Coreopsis verticillata
'Grandiflora' **3**

Salvia nemorosa
'Ostfriesland' **2**

Salvia ×*sylvestris*
'Schneehügel' **1**

EARLY BULBS

Narcissus
'Lemon Drops'
5–6 per area

Allium flavum
4–5 per area

Tulipa 'Spring Green'
3–5 per area

Allium cristophii
1–2 per area

Monet, *The Willows at Vétheuil*

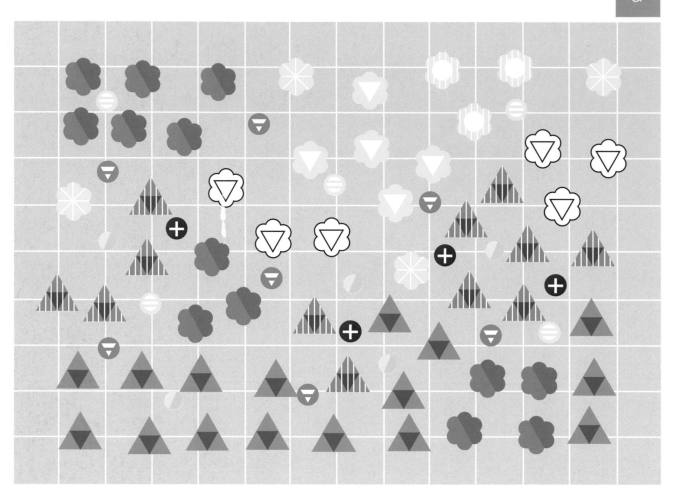

MAINTENANCE NOTES Be sure to remove old flower stems from the 'Happy Returns' daylily—it will promote rebloom. Don't cut back the 'Summer Beauty' allium; otherwise, you won't get to enjoy the nice burgundy-yellow autumn color of its flowering stems.

REMARKS The beautiful relationship between the seslerias and the carex in this planting—their tonal changes, texture, and growth habit—enhance all the other plants as they change through the season.

Sesleria caerulea **16**

Allium angulosum 'Summer Beauty' **13**

Sesleria autumnalis **12**

Anthericum ramosum **6**

Hemerocallis 'Happy Returns' **5**

Baptisia sphaerocarpa **4**

Solidago sphacelata 'Golden Fleece' **3**

EARLY BULBS

Narcissus 'Lemon Drops' **5–6 per area**

Allium carinatum subsp. *pulchellum* **4–5 per area**

Allium moly **4–5 per area**

Camassia quamash **4–5 per area**

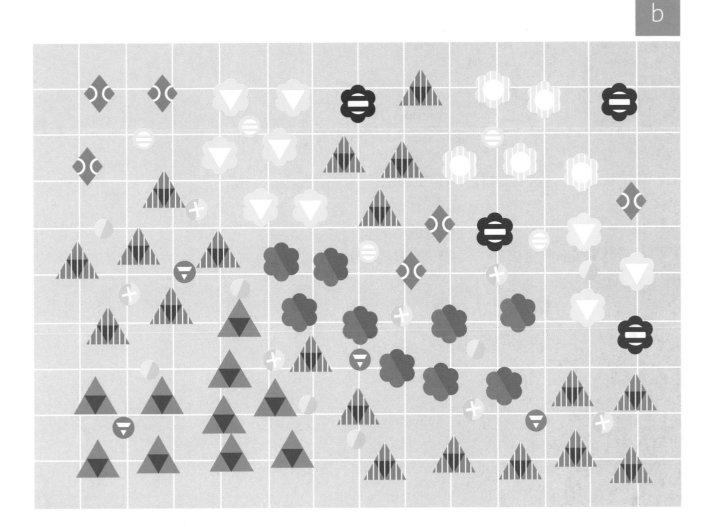

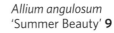

Sesleria autumnalis **19**

Allium angulosum 'Summer Beauty' **9**

Hemerocallis 'Happy Returns' **9**

Sesleria caerulea **10**

Carex flacca **6**

Solidago sphacelata 'Golden Fleece' **5**

Vernonia lettermannii 'Iron Butterfly' **4**

EARLY BULBS

Narcissus 'Lemon Drops' **5–6 per area**

Allium flavum **4–5 per area**

Allium moly **4–5 per area**

Camassia quamash **4–5 per area**

Pissarro, *Landscape at Pontoise*

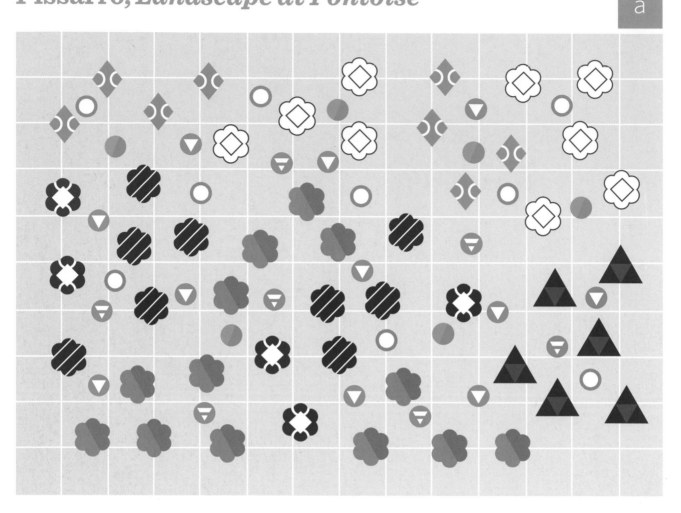

MAINTENANCE NOTES As the perovskia ages, it will cover the calamintha closest to it, which could be all right. Observe how they share the space. If a few calamintha disappear during the maturing of the garden, that's a good opportunity for spring bulbs. In three years you may need to thin the rhizomes of the carex. In a community, it's all about shared space.

REMARKS The violet spikes of the salvia attract most of the initial attention, as the blue foliage of the carex runs into and artistically meets the coppery, energetic foliage of the euphorbia.

Allium angulosum 'Summer Beauty' **13**

Calamintha nepeta **9**

Euphorbia polychroma 'Bonfire' **9**

Carex flacca **8**

Molinia caerulea subsp. *caerulea* 'Moorhexe' **6**

Salvia nemorosa 'Wesuwe' **5**

EARLY BULBS

Chionodoxa forbesii **6–7 per area**

Narcissus 'Jetfire' **5–6 per area**

Allium caeruleum **4–5 per area**

Camassia quamash **4–5 per area**

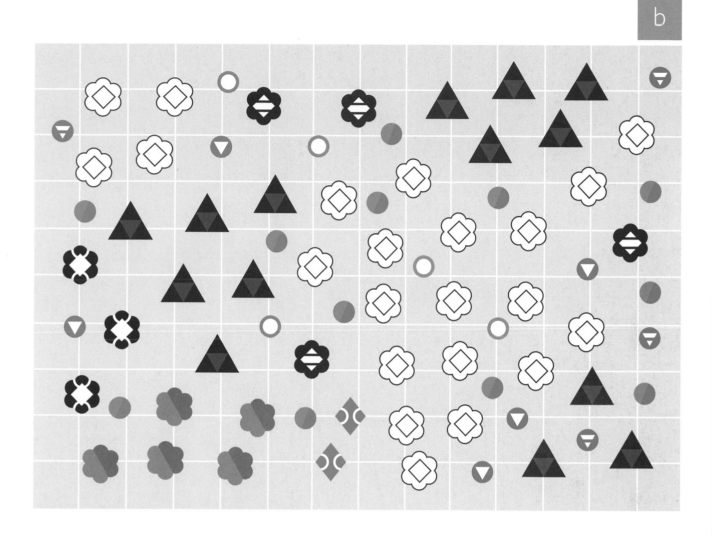

 Calamintha nepeta **22**

Molinia caerulea
subsp. *caerulea*
'Moorhexe' **14**

Allium angulosum
'Summer Beauty' **5**

Perovskia atriplicifolia
'Little Spire' **4**

Salvia nemorosa
'Wesuwe' **3**

Carex flacca **2**

Chionodoxa forbesii
6–7 per area

Narcissus 'Jetfire'
5–6 per area

Allium caeruleum
4–5 per area

Camassia quamash
4–5 per area

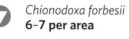

Hassam, *Flower Garden, Isles of Shoals*

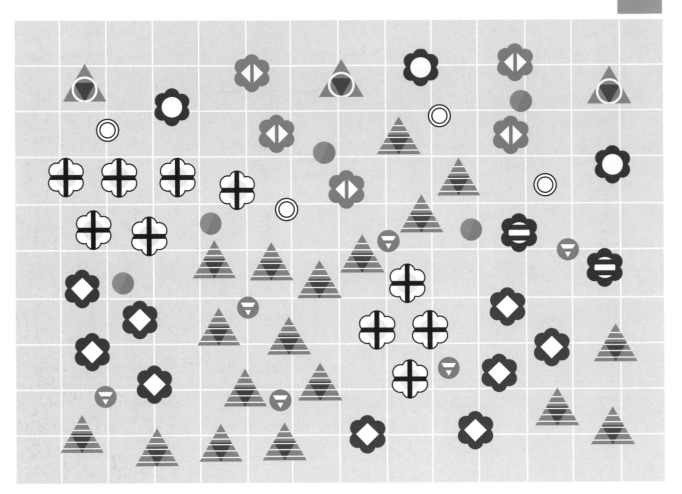

MAINTENANCE NOTES At the end of the year, observe the eupatorium. Does even 'Little Joe' look too big? If it seems out of scale with the other plants, you can divide it or root prune it push a tile spade through the roots at a 30-degree angle on all four sides; that should shorten the plant's development in the coming season.

REMARKS This planting is highlighted by the white echinacea, with its rich golden cones that later in the season turn blackish brown, strengthening the spiked seedheads of the agastache and stachys. The architecture of autumn!

Sporobolus heterolepis **18**

Echinacea purpurea 'Dwarf White Swan' **10**

Stachys officinalis 'Hummelo' **9**

Agastache 'Blue Fortune' **5**

Eupatorium dubium 'Little Joe' **3**

Panicum virgatum 'Northwind' **3**

Kalimeris incisa 'Blue Star' **2**

EARLY BULBS

Allium caeruleum **5–6 per area**

Narcissus 'Thalia' **4–6 per area**

Camassia quamash **4–5 per area**

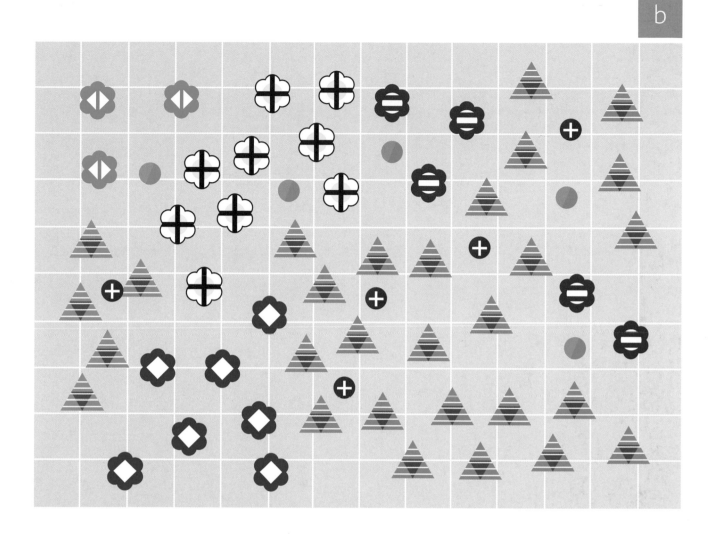

 Sporobolus
heterolepis **29**

 Echinacea purpurea
'Dwarf White Swan' **9**

Stachys officinalis
'Hummelo' **7**

 Kalimeris incisa
'Blue Star' **5**

Agastache
'Blue Fortune' **3**

EARLY BULBS

Allium caeruleum
5–6 per area

Allium carinatum
subsp. *pulchellum*
4–5 per area

van Gogh, *Garden with Flowers*

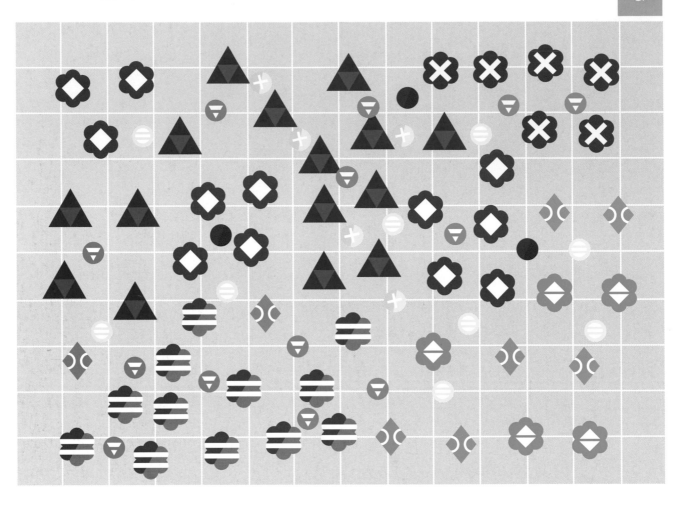

MAINTENANCE NOTES The carex will continue to spread by short rhizomes. Watch its relationship with neighboring plants. Also, though the salvia doesn't weaken easily, watch for its getting slightly crowded out in three to five years.

REMARKS The brilliant yellow flowers of the baptisia, along with the rich blue flowers of the salvia, are a highlight of early June; in July, the rich purple flowers of the stachys move to the fore, and later, the lavender clouds of limonium. It's truly a "garden with flowers."

▲ *Molinia caerulea* subsp. *caerulea* 'Moorhexe' **15**

≣ *Geranium sanguineum* 'Max Frei' **12**

✧ *Stachys officinalis* 'Hummelo' **12**

◈ *Carex flacca* **8**

✖ *Limonium latifolium* **6**

⬡ *Salvia* ×*sylvestris* 'Blauhügel' **5**

EARLY BULBS

▽ *Camassia quamash* **4–5 per area**

⊖ *Narcissus* 'Lemon Drops' **3–5 per area**

⊕ *Allium flavum* **3–4 per area**

● *Allium cristophii* **1–2 per area**

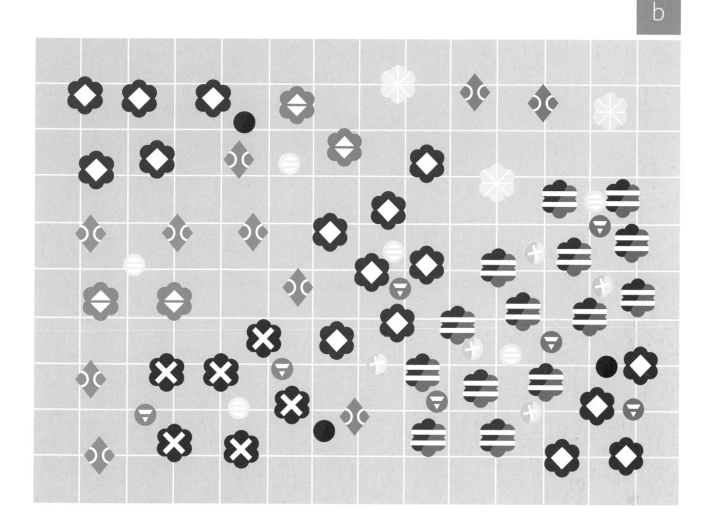

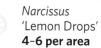

Stachys officinalis
'Hummelo' **16**

Geranium sanguineum
'Max Frei' **14**

Carex flacca **10**

Limonium latifolium **6**

Salvia ×sylvestris
'Blauhügel' **4**

Baptisia sphaerocarpa **3**

EARLY BULBS

Narcissus
'Lemon Drops'
4–6 per area

Camassia quamash
4–5 per area

Allium flavum
3–4 per area

Allium cristophii
1–2 per area

van Gogh, *Farms near Auvers*

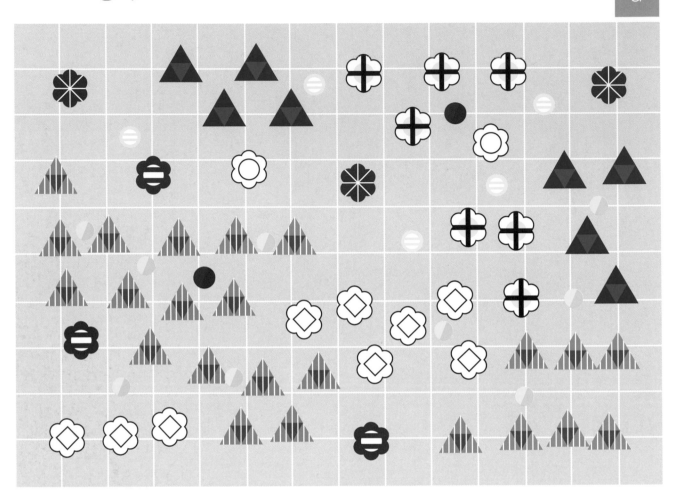

MAINTENANCE NOTES This garden will benefit from three to four supplemental waterings July through mid-August. Remember to get water deep into the root zone. The most valuable gardening skill is understanding the plant/water relationship, along with how you get water to your plants in a thoughtful manner.

REMARKS *Narcissus* 'Lemon Drops' and *Allium moly* add sunlit yellows to the green foliage of spring. In late summer the golden yellow flower spikes of the solidago will enhance the calamintha's clouds of white flowers and the bluish green foliage of the sesleria.

Sesleria autumnalis **23**

Calamintha nepeta **9**

Molinia caerulea subsp. *caerulea* 'Moorhexe' **8**

Echinacea purpurea 'Dwarf White Swan' **7**

Baptisia Purple Smoke' **3**

Kalimeris incisa 'Blue Star' **3**

Parthenium integrifolium **2**

EARLY BULBS

Narcissus 'Lemon Drops' **5–6 per area**

Allium moly **4–5 per area**

Allium cristophii **1–2 per area**

 Sesleria autumnalis **22**

 Molinia caerulea subsp. *caerulea* 'Moorhexe' **18**

Calamintha nepeta **10**

Solidago sphacelata 'Golden Fleece' **6**

Eupatorium dubium 'Baby Joe' **3**

EARLY BULBS

Narcissus 'Lemon Drops' **5–6 per area**

Allium flavum **4–5 per area**

Allium moly **4–5 per area**

Vuillard, *Window Overlooking the Woods*

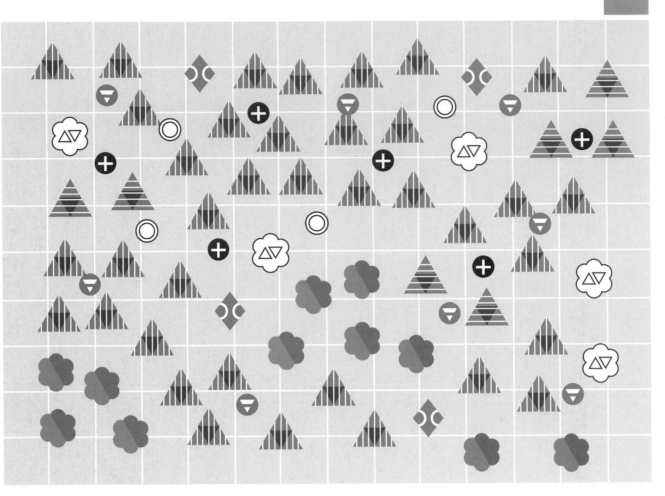

MAINTENANCE NOTES The plants in this pair of plans respect their space nicely. You want to watch how the grasses continue to relate to each other over time; it could be that you choose to add more blue carex foliage or change other elements.

REMARKS The tonal range changes from green to white and purple—an easy, relaxed movement through the season, and one that is, ideally, a happy reflection of all your other summer activities.

Sesleria autumnalis **37**

Allium angulosum 'Summer Beauty' **11**

Sporobolus heterolepis **7**

Carex flacca **4**

Gillenia trifoliata **5**

EARLY BULBS

Allium carinatum subsp. *pulchellum* **4–5 per area**

Camassia quamash **4–5 per area**

Narcissus 'Thalia' **4–5 per area**

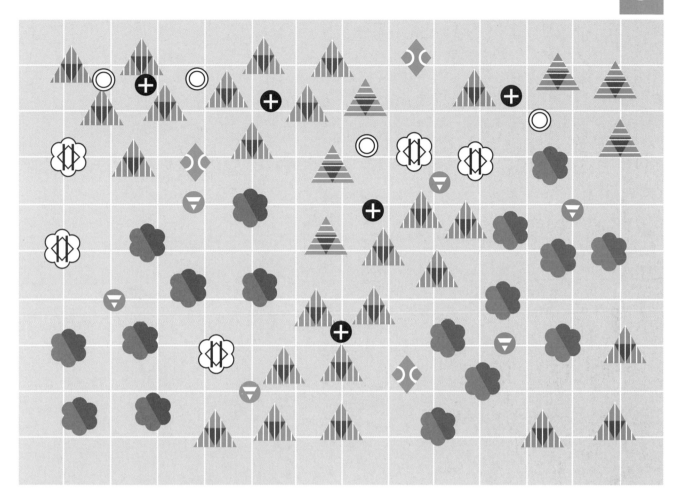

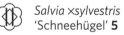

Sesleria autumnalis **27**

Allium angulosum
'Summer Beauty' **17**

Sporobolus heterolepis **6**

Salvia ×sylvestris
'Schneehügel' **5**

Carex flacca **3**

EARLY BULBS

Allium carinatum
subsp. *pulchellum*
4–5 per area

Camassia quamash
4–5 per area

Narcissus 'Thalia'
4–5 per area

Vuillard, *Young Woman in a Forest*

a

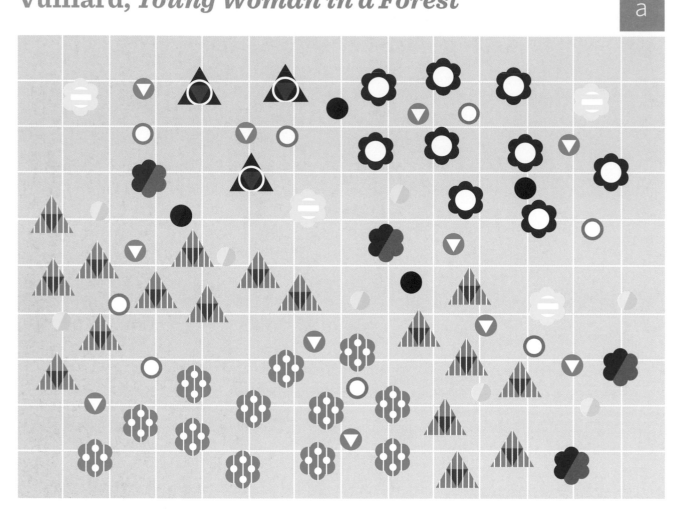

MAINTENANCE NOTES Here and in all communities that contain *Coreopsis verticillata* 'Grandiflora', keep an eye on how it coexists with the surrounding plants. You may or may not need to divide it every three to five years. Its relationship with other plants is up to you.

REMARKS In June the purple-blue of the amsonia and soft pink of the monarda flowers enliven the garden, eventually giving way to the subtle, contrasting textures and hits of golden yellow from the other plants.

Sesleria autumnalis **17**

Amsonia 'Blue Ice' **12**

Echinacea purpurea 'Rubinglow' **9**

Coreopsis verticillata 'Grandiflora' **4**

Geranium 'Tiny Monster' **4**

Panicum virgatum 'Heiliger Hain' or *P. v.* 'Ruby Ribbons' **3**

EARLY BULBS

Chionodoxa forbesii **5–6 per area**

Narcissus 'Jetfire' **5–6 per area**

Allium moly **4–5 per area**

Allium cristophii **1–2 per area**

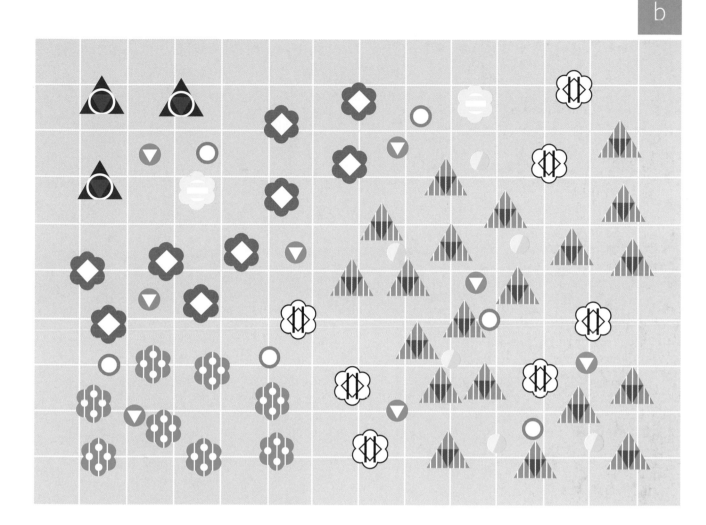

 Sesleria autumnalis **20**

Monarda bradburiana **9**

Amsonia 'Blue Ice' **8**

Salvia ×sylvestris
'Schneehügel' **7**

Panicum virgatum
'Heiliger Hain' or
P. v. 'Ruby Ribbons' **3**

Coreopsis verticillata
'Grandiflora' **2**

EARLY BULBS

Chionodoxa forbesii
5–6 per area

Narcissus 'Jetfire'
5–6 per area

Allium moly
4–5 per area

Pissarro, *The Wheel Barrow*

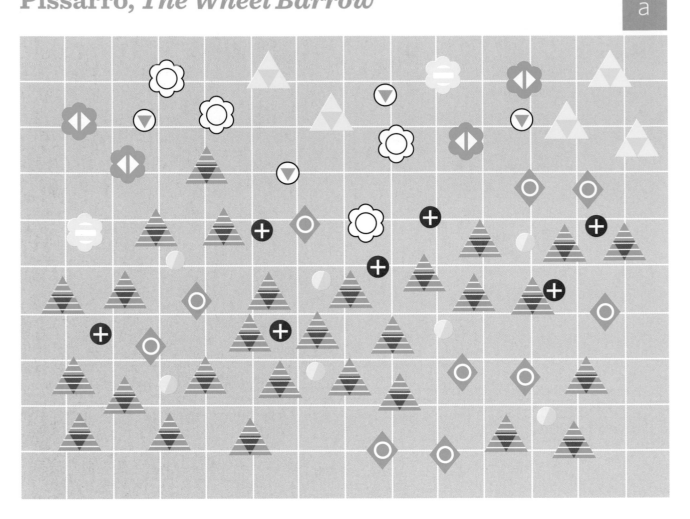

a

MAINTENANCE NOTES As the vernonia and sporobolus grow together in three to four years, notice how they blend together; if you want a higher accent of one or the other, garden in that direction. Undefined relationships can be exciting. As always, keep the balance of the coreopsis in mind.

REMARKS Textures sometimes produce deeper feelings than the more obvious dynamics of color. The sporobolus and carex (or sesleria, if that is your choice) are soft mounds of foliage in front of the white clouds of the parthenium and golden yellow flowers of the coreopsis.

Sporobolus heterolepis **28**

Carex swanii or *Sesleria autumnalis* **10**

Calamagrostis ×acutiflora 'Karl Foerster' **5**

Agastache 'Blue Fortune' **4**

Parthenium integrifolium **4**

Coreopsis verticillata 'Grandiflora' **2**

EARLY BULBS

Allium carinatum subsp. *pulchellum* **4–5 per area**

Allium moly **4–5 per area**

Tulipa 'Spring Green' **4–5 per area**

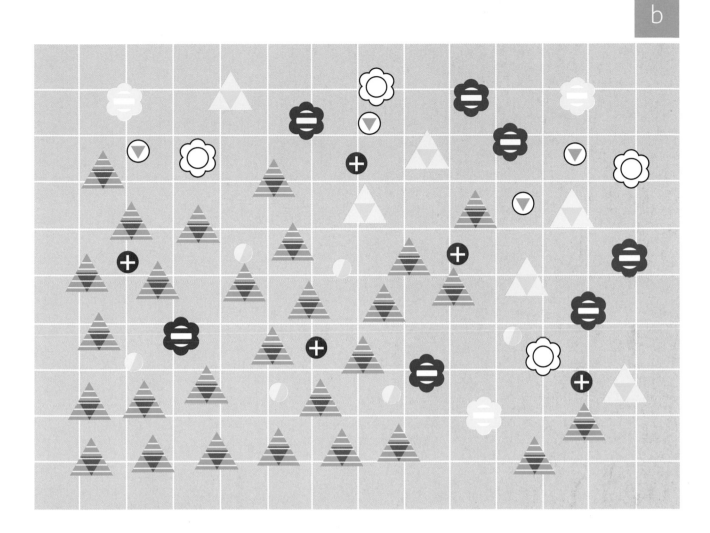

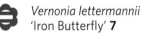 Sporobolus
heterolepis **27**

Vernonia lettermannii
'Iron Butterfly' **7**

Calamagrostis ×acutiflora
'Karl Foerster' **6**

Parthenium
integrifolium **4**

Coreopsis verticillata
'Grandiflora' **3**

EARLY BULBS

Allium carinatum
subsp. pulchellum
4–5 per area

Allium moly
4–5 per area

Tulipa 'Spring Green'
4–5 per area

Monet, *Water Lilies*, 1906

a

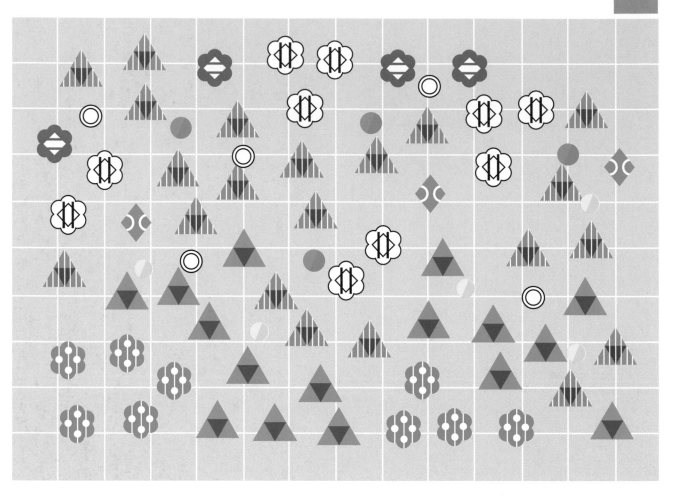

MAINTENANCE NOTES Plant the seslerias close; it's fine to snuggle them up—they've lived shoulder to shoulder for thousands of years. The amsonia and carex spread by short rhizomes; give them some attention. You may want to thin them as they grow into their neighbors. You could cut the salvia back right after flowering to promote heavy rebloom, or let the new blooms develop right through the older flowering stems.

REMARKS Collectively, this planting enhances all the beautiful characteristics of the individual plants, highlighting the blends and contrasts, whe ther they be of color, form, or texture. It has a very limpid, Impressionistic appearance.

Sesleria autumnalis **21**

Sesleria caerulea **16**

Salvia ×*sylvestris* 'Schneehügel' **10**

Amsonia 'Blue Ice' **9**

Carex flacca **3**

Nepeta subsessilis 'Cool Cat' **4**

EARLY BULBS

Allium caeruleum **5–6 per area**

Allium moly **4–5 per area**

Narcissus 'Thalia' **4–5 per area**

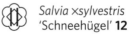

Sesleria autumnalis **18**

Sesleria caerulea **14**

Salvia ×sylvestris 'Schneehügel' **12**

Stachys officinalis 'Hummelo' **8**

Nepeta subsessilis 'Cool Cat' **4**

Carex flacca **3**

EARLY BULBS

Allium caeruleum **5–6 per area**

Allium moly **4–5 per area**

Narcissus 'Thalia' **4–5 per area**

Moments of Color

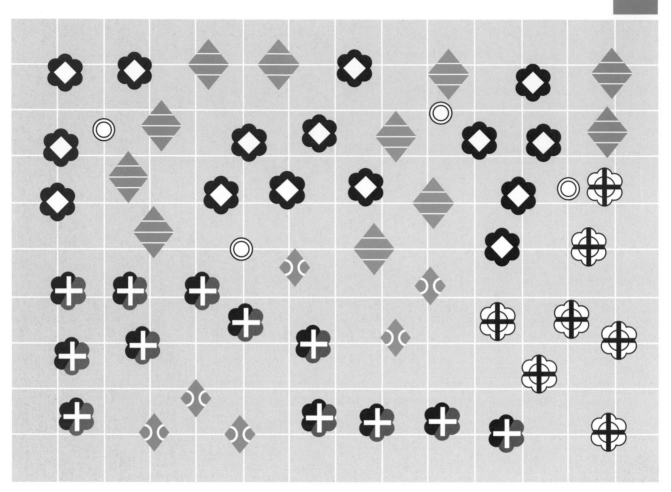

MAINTENANCE NOTES Cut down the previous year's foliage in March. Do not prune the geranium below the growing point—that will weaken the plant. After you've cut back the foliage, leave it around the plants.

REMARKS The grassy texture of the blue *Carex flacca* drifts and mingles with the medium green foliage of *C. shortiana*. In late May, the geranium brings magenta-pink color to the spring-green ground layer. In July, the vertical purple flowers of the stachys continue the movement of color within the planting, ending with the small white daisies of the eurybia. Throughout the season, the modest colors complement the textures.

Stachys officinalis 'Hummelo' **15**

Geranium macrorrhizum 'Bevan's Variety' **12**

Carex shortiana **11**

Eurybia divaricata **7**

Carex flacca **6**

EARLY BULBS

Narcissus 'Thalia' **4–5 per area**

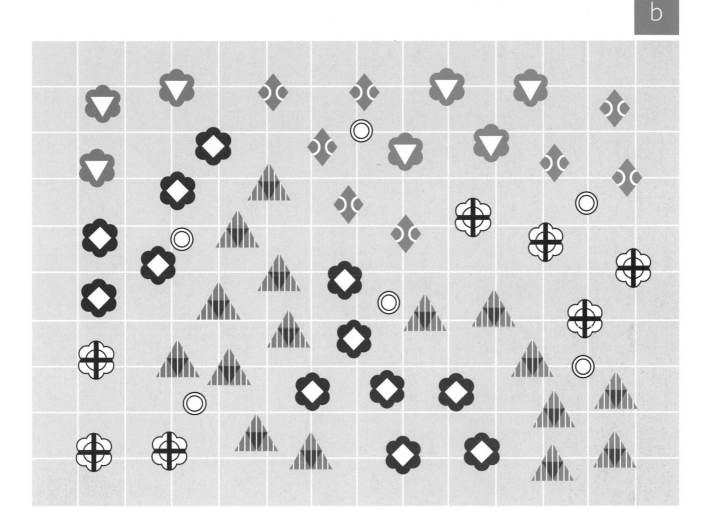

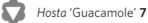 *Sesleria autumnalis* **16**

 Stachys officinalis ‘Hummelo’ **12**

 Carex flacca **8**

 Eurybia divaricata **7**

 Hosta ‘Guacamole’ **7**

EARLY BULBS

Narcissus ‘Thalia’ **4–5 per area**

The Drier Side

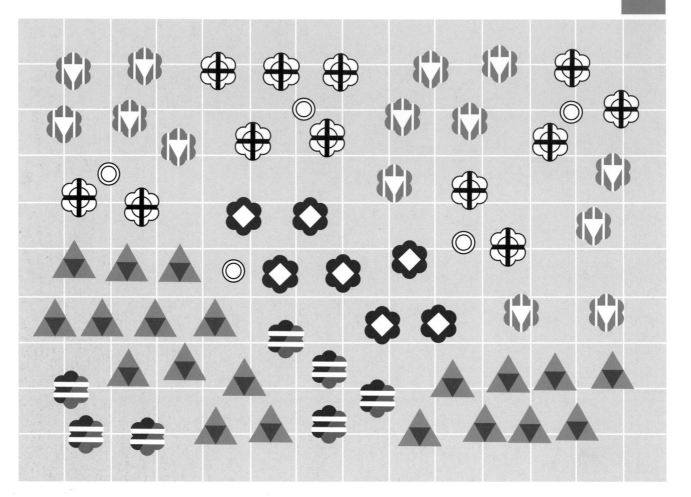

MAINTENANCE NOTES This is a very simple combination of plants that respect their space. The eurybia may reseed; remove the seedlings if you feel they create an imbalance in the planting. Water deeply two or three times during dry periods in July and August.

REMARKS From mid-May to early June, the sesleria, geranium, and narcissus will highlight the developing foliage, then in late summer the heuchera's white flower spires will mingle with the larger blue-green foliage of the hosta. Overall, there's nice moment-to-moment color and subtle changes of texture over the season.

Sesleria caerulea **20**

Hosta 'Halcyon' **14**

Eurybia divaricata **12**

Geranium sanguineum 'Max Frei' **7**

Stachys officinalis 'Hummelo' **7**

EARLY BULBS

Narcissus 'Thalia'
4–5 per area

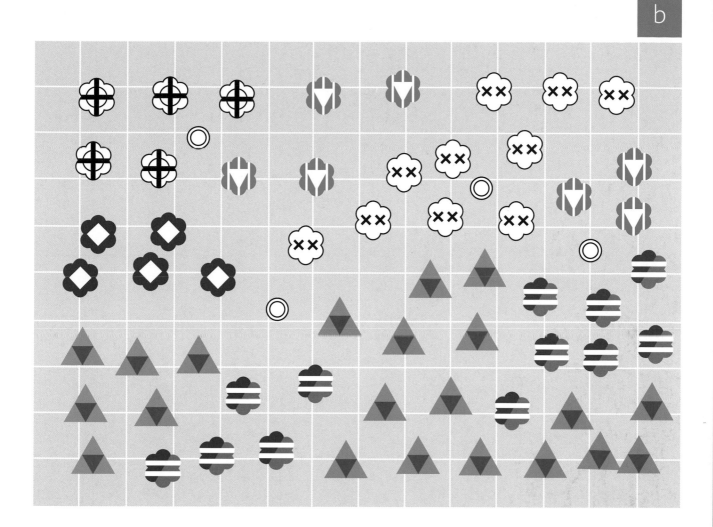

 *Sesleria caerulea* **21**

Geranium sanguineum
'Max Frei' **12**

 Heuchera villosa
'Autumn Bride' **10**

Hosta 'Halcyon' **7**

Eurybia divaricata **5**

Stachys officinalis
'Hummelo' **5**

EARLY BULBS

Narcissus 'Thalia'
4–5 per area

Sturdy Textures

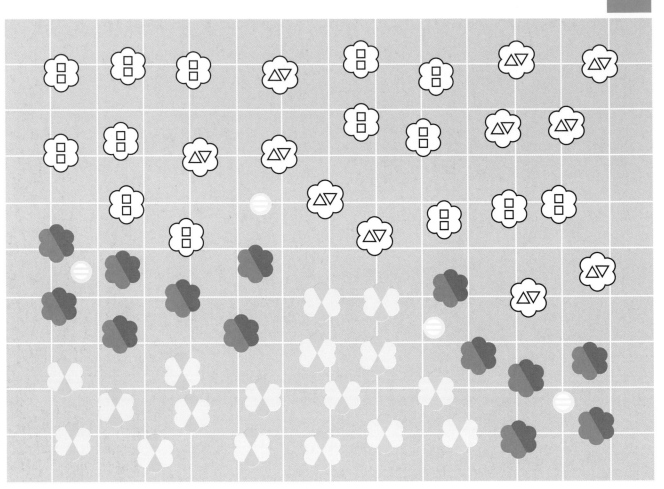

MAINTENANCE NOTES Cut the planting back in March and leave the debris around the plants. At this point the epimedium foliage might still look nice; nevertheless, you should cut it back to encourage strong flowering. During the blooming period, beautiful new foliage will cover the plant, hiding the fading flowers. Assess the gillenia and thalictrum relationship they both reseed; keep a nice balance. Water deeply four or five times in July and August if the weather is exceptionally dry.

REMARKS The soft yellow flowers of the epimedium accent the lacy texture of the thalictrum and the strappy, rich green foliage of the allium. In July the large white flowers of the echinacea rise just above the thalictrum and grassy foliage of the carexes. This is a pleasant planting to walk by, or through repeat it, a mirrored flip, its fronts lining either side of path.

 Epimedium ×versicolor 'Sulphureum' **17**

Thalictrum dioicum **14**

Allium angulosum 'Summer Beauty' **13**

Gillenia trifoliata **11**

EARLY BULBS

Narcissus 'Lemon Drops' **4–5 per area**

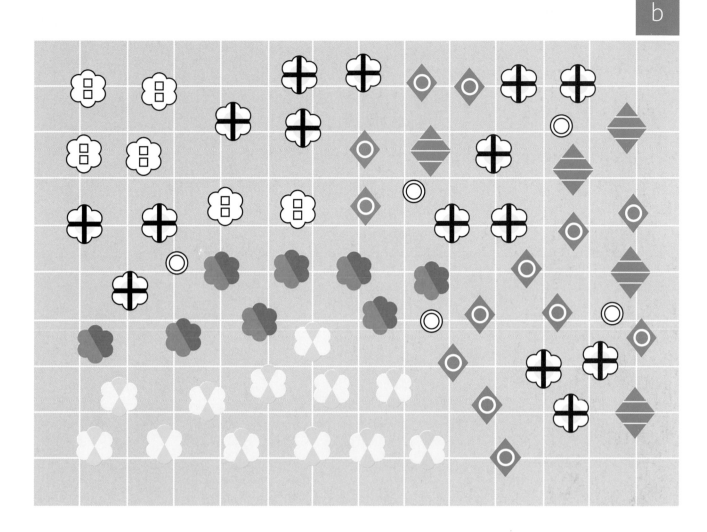

 Echinacea purpurea 'Dwarf White Swan' **15**

 Carex swanii **13**

 Epimedium ×*versicolor* 'Sulphureum' **12**

 Allium angulosum 'Summer Beauty' **8**

Carex shortiana **5**

EARLY BULBS

Narcissus 'Thalia' **4–5 per area**

Kinetic Textures

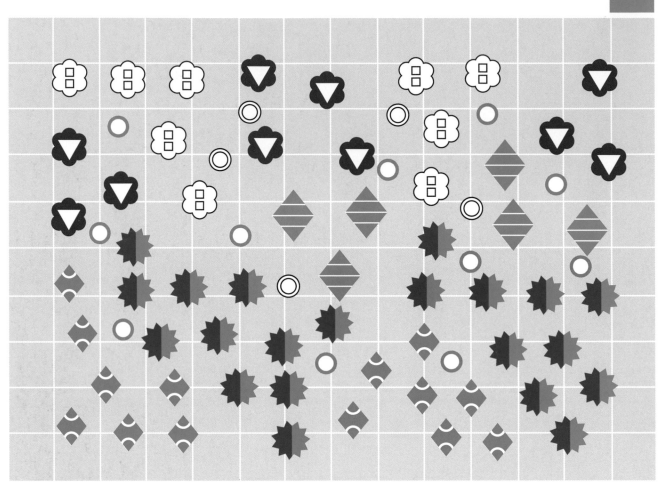

MAINTENANCE NOTES The dryopteris and carexes will grow together snugly and live well. Be aware of moisture conditions in late June and July. If rainfall has been scanty, watering deeply would be a good idea. Cut the planting back in March, leaving the debris around the plants.

REMARKS The dainty, pink and white flowers of the low, mounded epimedium float casually in front of and between the developing fronds of the polystichum. At the same time, the powder-blue and chartreuse leaves of the two hostas are emerging strongly, covering the ground by mid-June. The eurybia forms a low layer of green in summer, then sends up soft clouds of white flowers in September.

Dryopteris marginalis **21**

Carex grisea **14**

Hosta 'August Moon' **10**

Thalictrum dioicum **9**

Carex shortiana **6**

EARLY BULBS

Narcissus 'Jetfire'
4–5 per area

Narcissus 'Thalia'
4–5 per area

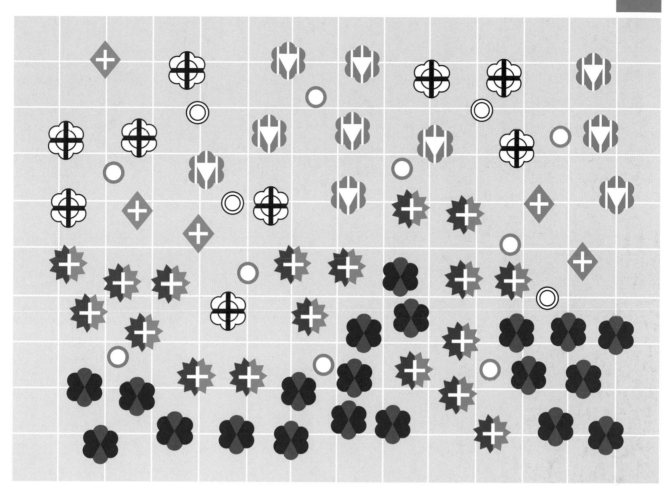

 Epimedium ×rubrum **20**

 Polystichum acrostichoides **18**

 Hosta 'Halcyon' **10**

 Eurybia divaricata **9**

 Carex sprengelii **5**

EARLY BULBS

Narcissus 'Jetfire'
4–5 per area

Narcissus 'Thalia'
4–5 per area

Variations on the Theme of Leaf

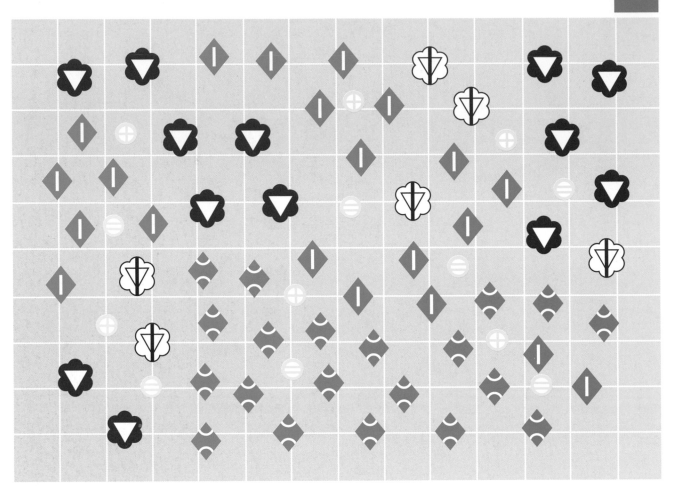

MAINTENANCE NOTES Cut the planting back in March and leave the debris around the plants. The maianthemum will spread by rhizomes, forming 2-foot colonies in five to six years. You can dig some out in April and plant the divisions in a new location, or just let them spread, removing only those that disrupt the style of the planting.

REMARKS The geraniums will grow together nicely, creating a textured river of gray-green foliage moving through the chartreuse of the hostas. In late May the geraniums will bloom magenta-pink, lasting through June. An enlivened moment, bringing textural foliage into summer.

Carex grisea **20**

Carex brevior **19**

Hosta 'August Moon' **13**

Maianthemum racemosum **6**

EARLY BULBS

Narcissus 'February Gold'
4–5 per area

Narcissus 'Lemon Drops'
4–5 per area

Carex grisea **18**

Geranium macrorrhizum 'Bevan's Variety' **17**

Carex brevior **15**

Hosta 'August Moon' **10**

EARLY BULBS

Narcissus 'February Gold' **4–5 per area**

Narcissus 'Thalia' **4–5 per area**

A Carex Matrix

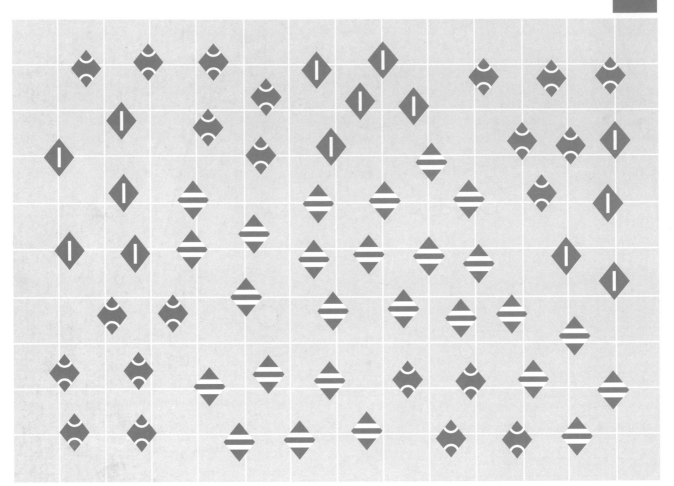

MAINTENANCE NOTES The carexes are planted together tightly, creating a closed community that limits weed competition and that can be enhanced as time and finances permit. See chapter 5 for other sedges to add. In March, cut the entire planting back with a mulching mower, leaving the debris among the plants.

REMARKS A carex matrix provides a soothing scene of contrasting foliage, filling shady areas, minimizing weed competition, and constantly adding organic matter back to the soil. Keep in mind that carexes can be planted around trees and shrubs as a living mulch.

Carex grisea **22**

 Carex bromoides **26**

Carex brevior **14**

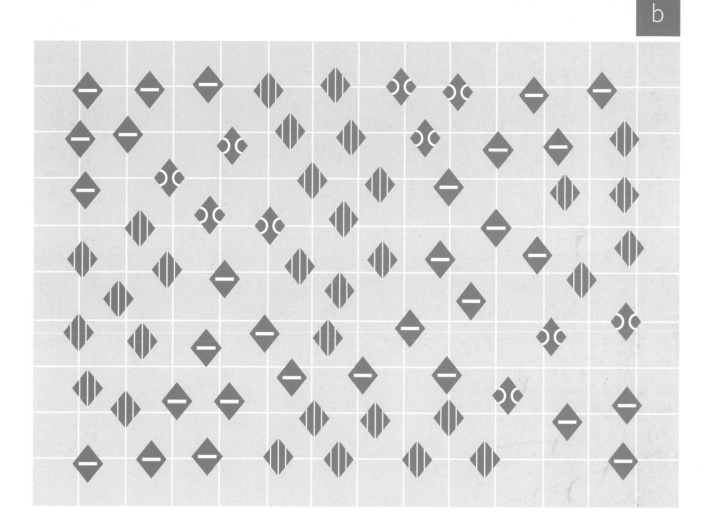

Carex pensylvanica **30**

Carex montana **31**

Carex flacca **10**

Another Carex Matrix

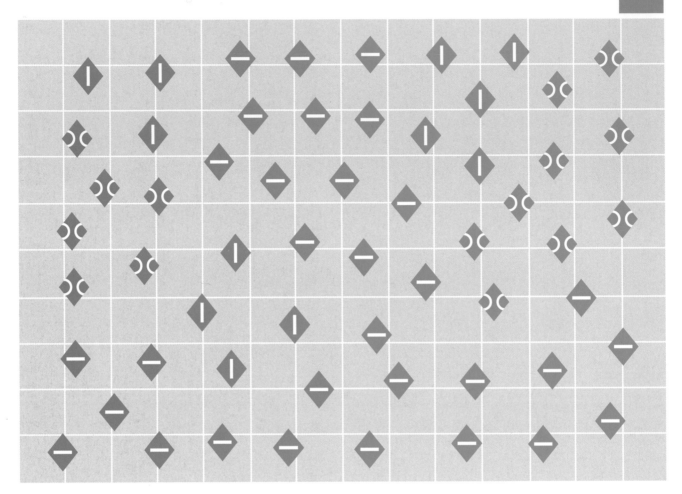

MAINTENANCE NOTES The *Carex flacca* in particular will become larger if they receive more light. If you add flowering and structural plants to the matrix, some of the sedges will need to be removed, allowing the enhancement plants the opportunity to establish. In March, cut the entire planting back with a mulching mower, leaving the debris among the plants.

REMARKS This carex matrix can function as a transition planting from light shade to sun, promoting garden continuity. Both matrixes can be woven together, creating an extensive yet diverse ground layer. "Repeat as necessary."

Carex pensylvanica **31**

Carex flacca **15**

Carex brevior **12**

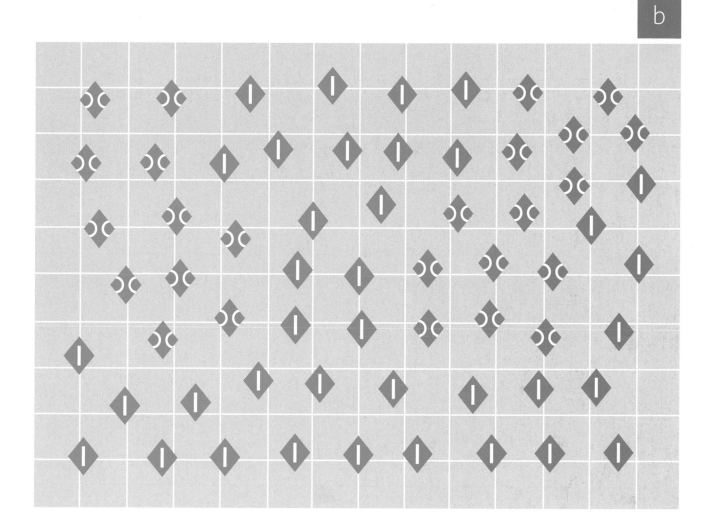

Carex brevior **37**

Carex flacca **25**

Substance, Strength, and Texture in Green

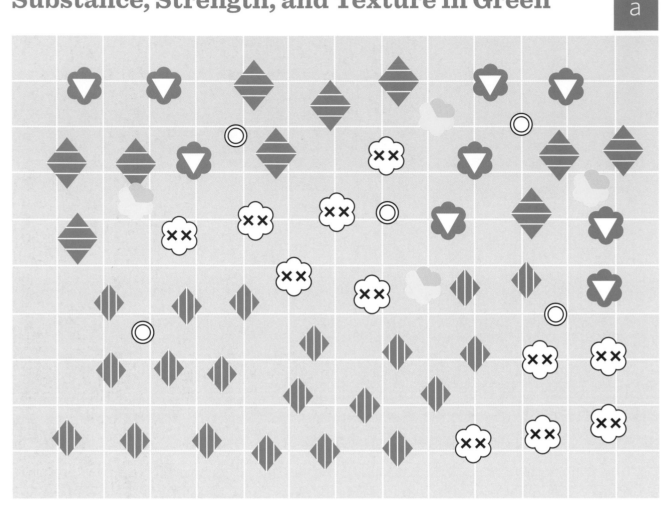

MAINTENANCE NOTES Cut the plants back in March, leaving the debris around the plants. Do not prune the heuchera below the area of new growth—that will kill it. The ferns will enjoy their snug spacing, and the asarum will increase, growing together and covering the soil. In early June the mertensia foliage will start to yellow; when it becomes a distraction, remove it. In time the mertensia will reseed—you can decide how this fits into the dynamics of the garden.

REMARKS This is a sensual planting mix, consisting of the large, soft green leaves of the heuchera, the grassy, bright green of *Carex montana*, and the glossy apple-green of *Hosta* 'Guacamole'. It's a foliar community worth repeating throughout a shaded site.

Carex montana **20**

Heuchera villosa 'Autumn Bride' **11**

Carex shortiana **10**

Hosta 'Guacamole' **9**

 Mertensia virginica **4**

EARLY BULBS

Narcissus 'Thalia' **4–5 per area**

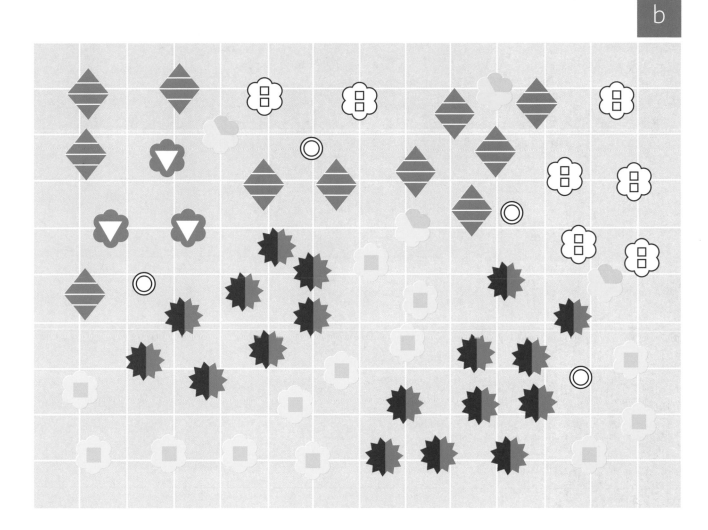

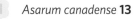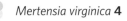

Dryopteris marginalis **18**

Carex shortiana **11**

Asarum canadense **13**

Thalictrum dioicum **7**

Hosta 'Guacamole' **3**

Mertensia virginica **4**

EARLY BULBS

Narcissus 'Thalia'
4–5 per area

The Fernery

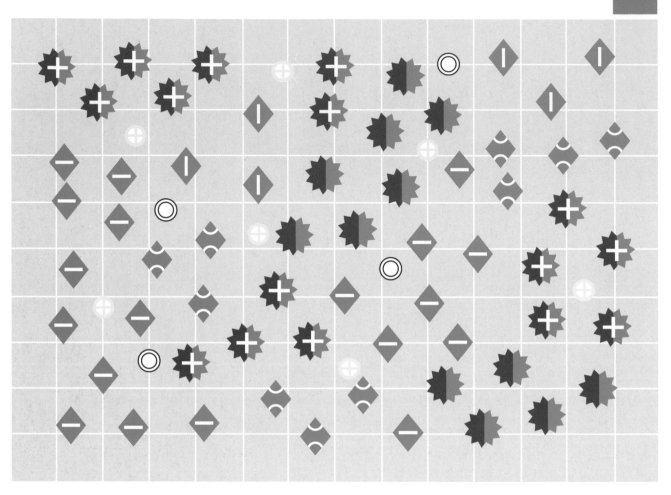

MAINTENANCE NOTES The carexes will knit together along with the ferns, creating a closed community that will greatly reduce weed competition. Cut everything back in March with a mulching mower, leaving the debris around the plants.

REMARKS This grouping is characterized by soft-textured contrasting foliage. The ferns drift through the sedges, creating islands of upright fronds in a sea of narrow, grassy foliage. This community is very receptive to being inter-planted with perennials that will grow through their tight foliage; some possibilities are *Geranium maculatum*, *Mertensia virginica*, and *Caulophyllum thalictroides*.

 Carex pensylvanica **19**

Polystichum acrostichoides **16**

Dryopteris marginalis **12**

 *Carex grisea* **10**

Carex brevior **6**

EARLY BULBS

Narcissus 'February Gold' **4–5 per area**

Narcissus 'Thalia' **4–5 per area**

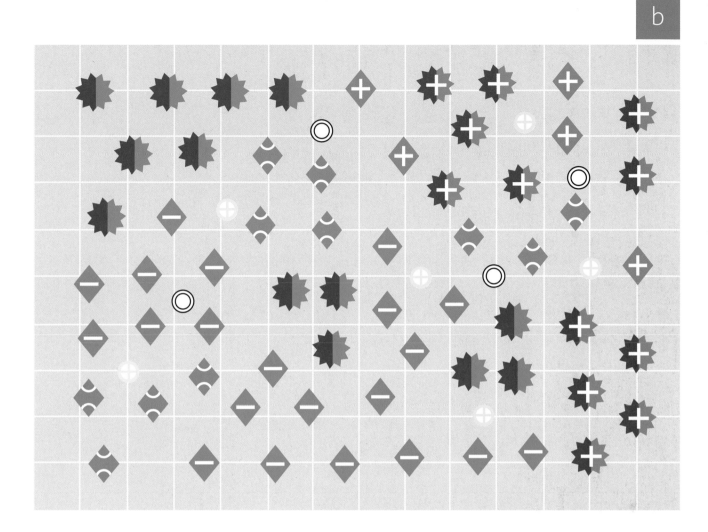

Carex pensylvanica **21**	**EARLY BULBS**
	Narcissus
Dryopteris marginalis **13**	'February Gold'
	4–5 per area
Polystichum *acrostichoides* **12**	
	Narcissus 'Thalia'
Carex grisea **11**	**4–5 per area**
Carex sprengelii **5**	

Chapter 7

Creating Your Own Plant Communities

Perennial plant relationships all have certain traits in common. If you understand these traits, it should be possible to create and nurture your own plant community, using the perennials featured in this book or other plants with which you are familiar. As always, try not to expect immediate results—it's much more important to have an overall set of goals and objectives. Taking your time is also less of a drain on your pocketbook and minimizes your chances of making a big mistake.

Before you forge ahead, remember these important points from earlier chapters:

- You have to know the plant! Without plant knowledge, nothing can happen.
- You have to know your site conditions.
- You have to own your commitment to care and maintenance.
- You have to be sure you're telling yourself the truth.

In fact, it would be a good idea to review chapter 1 five times. Why five? Because it's too easy to go over something once and feel you're done. That one-time view may not allow you to completely take in the methods offered or to properly value the thinking behind them. Continue to ask the questions that get you closer to all plants. And since we're on the subject, also review the notion of plant dynamics in chapter 4, particularly the discussion of the qualities and characteristics that enable plants to build associations and live well together. Knowing the structure and growth habit of the plant, you'll be able to create mixed communities based on "selection percentages" for each plant. This in turn is based on the plant's growth habit, height, and how rapidly it reaches that height during the growing season.

Let's look at some specific examples. Remember: start simple. If you put too many different plants together, the result will look messy and you'll have a hard time figuring out how to care for the garden community. Believe me—I've done it.

A plant community isn't a one-note samba. It's about composition. Do you listen to music because of a favorite note?

Example 1

We'll start with *Allium angulosum* 'Summer Beauty' and *Sesleria autumnalis*. Both plants have a vertical/mounding growth habit, being only slightly taller than wide. However, the allium reaches its maximum height sooner, by late June, when it begins to flower. The sesleria will be slightly shorter at this time, reaching its top seasonal height as it begins to bloom in early to mid-August. Each plant has characteristics that enhance the other: the darker, wider foliage of the allium contrasts nicely with the narrow foliage of the sesleria. Also, they both live in average to slightly drier soils and respect their space. By the third year, they will have grown into each other; however, they will not inhibit each other's development. In four to five years, if you wish, you can thin one or the other based on the percentage of each plant you selected and how you placed them in relation to each other.

But we're getting ahead of ourselves. Let's assume that the space you want to plant is 50 square feet (5 feet by 10 feet). There are three questions to ask yourself. How many plants total do you need to plant that area? What percentage of each would you need to create the composition? And how should you place them?

First, let's determine how many plants you'll need. Note: you're not planting right up to the edges of the bed—you need to leave a foot of bare soil all the way around to allow for the plants' growth—so you're actually planting about 36 square feet (4 feet by 9 feet). The plants' growth habit suggests that they should be spaced 15 inches apart.

Here is a simple formula to determine how many plants are needed, based on spacing. If you are using 15-inch spacing on center, multiply 15 × 15—that will give you 225 square inches. Next multiply 12 × 12—that gives you 144 square inches (the square foot is your baseline in all these calculations). Now divide 225 square inches by 144 square inches—that equals 1.56. This number—1.56—is what you use when you want to determine how many plants are necessary for the area you're planting (in this case, 36 square feet) using 15-inch centers. So, divide 36 square feet by 1.56, for 15-inch spacing of the plants: that's 23 plants. This formula works for any size plot and with any spacing. If you want 18-inch centers, say, just multiply: 18 × 18 = 324, and 324 divided by 144 (the same square foot baseline) equals 2.25. Sticking with the 36-square-foot example, you would again divide 36, this time by 2.25, for a total of 16 plants.

Next, let's settle on what percentage of each to use. This requires a combination of art and plant awareness. Would you like the experience to be more colorful or more textural? Let's go with what most folks decide on: more

color. So we'll begin with 60% allium (14 plants) and 40% sesleria (nine plants).

Now we will create the composition. Here's what you need to think about when placing the plants: if you surround one allium with several seslerias, the allium will decline, weakened by the surrounding, maturing grasses. This won't happen rapidly; it will just peter out within the grasses. Let's reverse the situation. Let's say we plant a sesleria and surround it with alliums. The grass will do well for a longer period of time because its narrow foliage can capture sunlight easily; it isn't troubled by the dominant foliage of the allium. So in this case, keep the alliums in groups of three, four, or five. I usually place the alliums first and weave the grasses around them. The alliums are the accent plants for this community.

Now get out some grid paper, draw a 5- by 10-foot rectangle, and place the 14 alliums and nine seslerias. But don't do just one grid. Do five. Get a feeling for how many combinations you can make with just two plants within 50 square feet of space using the same percentage for each plant (60% allium and 40% sesleria). Then choose the arrangement you like best and ask yourself why. What makes that your style?

Now do five more grids and change the percentages. When you do these additional diagrams, remove some of either the allium or sesleria and add one, two, or three more plants—try two *Coreopsis verticillata* 'Grandiflora' or six *Echinacea purpurea* 'Rubinglow', or five *Salvia nemorosa* 'Wesuwe'—always totaling 23 plants within the 50 square feet, of course. Notice how it affects the aesthetics of your groupings and their developmental and maintenance practices. When do you have too many different plants?

As you keep adding different plants, going from two or four kinds to eight or 10 within the 50 square feet, does the pattern get too eclectic, do you lose a sense of rhythm? Does it get messy? This feeling of composition you have to develop. At one time I had a "plant collection" planting. I may have had 14 different plants, one or two of each in 50 square feet. It became difficult to care for. Some grew too tall in relation to the others, and some too short. Others spread by rhizomes, much too fast. *Lysimachia clethroides* spread endlessly, and *Sorghastrum nutans* seeded into everything. That's when I began to think about using plants that respect their space and live well intimately. That's when I recognized the importance of composition and having a style.

Keep practicing the grid diagrams and changing the percentages of plants. Don't think you're done! Practice is important; there is no way to learn and experience this in a few days. When you draw your grids, take them seriously. Study each diagram and try to imagine how the actual planting will look—the first year, and five years later. Keep questioning yourself. How will these plants live together? What will I have to do to take care of this planting as the years move on? Do I want that amount of work? As the patterns become more representative of your style, you can begin increasing the size of the area and the number of plants; or, if you're working with a limited space, you can reduce the size of the area, creating small garden-enhancement grids that can be added to your existing garden. These smaller grids—say, 3 feet by 4 feet—can contain one plant species that lives well in its own company, or a couple of plants on a first date, interplanted together.

Up to now you have been doing all this planning on paper: you're visualizing plants and their initial planting space, and understanding how they mature and live together. You haven't bought a single plant or prepared one bed. But don't minimize the value of creating and interpreting your diagrams. All those mornings, afternoons, and evenings of forethought are not for nothing. When it comes time to purchase plants and prepare the area for planting, you'll go into it knowing everything you need to know:

- How many of each sort of plant you'll need.
- How the plants will mature and live together.
- Where to place each plant within the available space.
- How involved you'll need to be, both in the planting's initial nurturing and in its ongoing maintenance.

Because of the dynamics of plants, weather, and people, you will be taken by surprise sometimes, and the interjection "Huh!" will frequently punctuate your gardening adventures. That's alright. Remember, it's not only the plants that are nurtured, growing, and maturing: you're

A modest percentage of *Salvia nemorosa* 'Wesuwe' is a welcome, distinctly vertical addition to this plant community.

forever learning, acquiring knowledge and confidence, becoming an artist. You're patience as a grounded person and thoughtful caregiver is rewarded. All because you got to know some plants—see? aren't you lucky! And remember, if you want to, you can change the planting. Now you're gardening!

Example 2

Here's another plant community for us to work through together. Let's use *Perovskia atriplicifolia* 'Little Spire' and *Echinacea purpurea* 'Virgin'. Again, we'll start with a 50-square-foot garden space.

The perovskia has soft gray foliage with narrow panicles of small lilac-blue flowers in July. It grows 32 to 38

When the number of plants needed for the two example plant communities was established, the total square footage of the area was not used because planting is not appropriate on the edge of a freestanding bed. But! Perhaps the plan is for your new plant community to be connected to an established planting, to enhance the overall garden. In this case, your calculations for the area to be planted should incorporate the square footage of the new diagram up to the very edge of the side that connects to the older planting. That additional square footage in the new diagram will give you enough plants to connect the two plantings together.

inches tall and can get 18 to 24 inches wide in three to five years; so, although it has a vertical/upright growth habit, it does take up quite a bit of space horizontally by early July. (If you use the straight species *Perovskia atriplicifolia*, the plant will get slightly taller and will lean over more when it begins flowering, giving it an even wider appearance.) *Echinacea purpurea* 'Virgin' gets to be 26 to 32 inches tall by July when it begins flowering and 12 to 14 inches wide in three to five years. The echinacea too has a vertical/upright habit but is slightly shorter than the perovskia. The echinacea's strongly horizontal white flower petals, which encircle the cone, and its dense flowering stems blend beautifully into the slightly lax gray-blue, vertical flowering stems of the perovksia. It's quite nice!

Let's look again at how to determine the spacing for these two plants. We'll rely on the same formulas, but these plants are taller and take up more space than the allium and sesleria. Given their size, these two plants should initially have more space to grow into but we still want them modestly blending together. So let's work with 18-inch centers. The earlier calculations showed you how to get the number 2.25. Since you have a 50-square-foot bed not bordered on any sides by other plants, we again have 36 square feet of planting space. To arrive at 18-inch-on-center spacing, divide 36 by 2.25; that will give you the number of plants needed to fill the space. Again, 36 divided by 2.25 is 16.

Now let's determine the percentage of each plant. The question is one of growth rate and habit: which plant will fill the most space in three to five years, and how? The perovskia grows wider, and its tall stems can be a little lax. The echinacea grows narrower and remains more vertical. Since the perovskia will take up more space, a lower percentage should be used in the composition. Let's use perovskia at 30% and the echinacea at 70%. We will definitely have more visual impact from the echinacea, yet a good representation of the perovskia as well. Remember, as time goes by the balance will change, and you may be fine with more or less echinacea or perovskia. As long as the planting is healthy and has no open gaps, the evolved combination could be fine, or you may have to remove some perovskia and add echinacea, or vice versa, to maintain the initial balance. That's your decision as the artist in the garden.

For this 50-square-foot planting 30% perovskia would be five plants and 70% echinacea would be 11 plants. The perovskia will be larger and is more structural; it should be placed on the grid diagram first, and then the echinacea sited through the perovskia.

Review your initial grid and diagram a few more, keeping in mind how placement affects relationships. Again, sense the harmony of the patterns and why each appeals to you. Now, as before, add one, two, three, and four different plants to the diagram, always keeping the total number of plants at 16. Notice how expanding the variety of plants changes the aesthetics and development of the entire planting, which in turn has an impact on the maintenance. You may decide that adding different plants to this grouping isn't worth it, since they may require too much additional care to justify the new style.

Extra credit and review

Here are some plants to use to develop more practice diagrams. Try incorporating them into the various-sized planting spaces suggested for each selection. Again, review the formal plant descriptions in chapter 5 to determine their growth rate and growth habit, and to discover some options for plants you may want to place them with. Write down how they may grow together and what care will be necessary in the next five years. See how your goal of living comfortably with them affects your choice of plants.

> *Eupatorium dubium* 'Little Joe':
> 5 × 5 ft.; 4 × 8 ft; 5 × 12 ft.
> *Eurybia divaricata*:
> 3 × 8 ft.; 4 × 8 ft.; 6 × 6 ft.
> *Geranium sanguineum* 'Max Frei':
> 4 × 6 ft.; 5 × 8 ft.; 3 × 15 ft.
> *Hosta* 'Halcyon':
> 3 × 5 ft.; 4 × 7 ft., 6 × 12 ft.
> *Kalimeris incisa* 'Blue Star':
> 3 × 5 ft.; 4 × 7 ft.; 5 × 10 ft.
> *Panicum virgatum* 'Northwind':
> 4 × 6 ft.; 3 × 15 ft.; 7 × 15 ft.
> *Parthenium integrifolium*:
> 3 × 5 ft.; 4 × 12 ft.; 7 × 15 ft.
> *Stachys officinalis* 'Hummelo':
> 4 × 4 ft.; 3 × 10 ft.; 5 × 7 ft.

When you have taken time to create these small plant communities, you will be surprised at how much more you have learned. Developing relationships is the cornerstone of healthy living, in the garden and in life.

This blend of *Geranium sanguineum* 'Album' and *G. s.* 'Max Frei' both live well growing into each other and faithfully cover the soil early, outcompeting the germinating weed seeds. Form and function!

Here is the simplest thought of all to hold in mind, before you attempt to create your own plant community, whatever its size. You have read it a number of times. It's the essence of the book: know the plant! Here are some others.

- Start simply. You can always add more planting space and plants.
- Start with the plants in chapter 5. In the last 34 years, I've killed many plants five times over. These plants have lived; they have character and are very forgiving, allowing you time to figure them out.
- If you find other plants that inspire you, plant them in an evaluation bed and study them. How does each potential fit into your style and practice of gardening? There will always be new plants. Know why and how that tempting new introduction could make your garden better.

- The most important things to know about any plant you're considering as part of your palette are its growth rate and growth habit. Whatever spacing you use (and often you may mix them), everything will depend on how big the plant gets and how fast it gets there.
- For help with percentages, which plant takes up the most space? That generally would be the plant at the lower percentage.
- For help when placing the plants, site the stronger, architectural plants first and then the mounding, modest plants.
- Practice. Keep putting plants on grids and anticipate what will happen, the first year into the fifth. Write down your thoughts, then evaluate them.
- Be patient! If you want too much too quickly, you fail— yourself and your planting. The only immediate things we need are inhaling and exhaling.
- Be flexible and adaptable. Everything is movable. If one plant or a small group doesn't look right to you or requires more care than you can give, just move the plants into a better situation.
- Learn from the garden plans in this book. Watch how

they grow together, and note how involved you are in their care. In a short time, you may see some changes you want to make, and you will be in a position to know why and how they should be accomplished.

- Learn from your perceived mistakes; gardening, like life, always involves change.
- There is no finished moment. Your planting will always need you.
- Share what you learn. And have some fun!

I want to end this important chapter by addressing and acknowledging the intangible question of composition. Beyond knowing maintenance, you have to appreciate composition. How do you determine what plant you choose and what plant to put it with? How do you know what you like and what you don't like? And can you put your finger on why?

Composition is subjective. It's all your feelings telling you at the same time what is beautiful—to you. Composition is then pausing and waiting until those feelings level off and then creating an image of the overall experience. Composition is being open and alive and then expressing

Have I enjoyed something beyond flowers in fullest bloom? The answer is too easy, of course. In late summer and autumn, beauty is the timely shift of palette that pushes us into winter.

that vitality. Composition is the only way to take all the plants that move you emotionally, place them together, understanding their dynamic capabilities, and let them go. As they get on with living, you watch, react, watch, react. And through time, as your garden evolves, you and all the people who see it live with beauty. Composition is randomness filtered through a human mind and released into the world—interpreted, critiqued, cried for, imitated, sold, found, loved, and mourned, in passing. It's one way to interpret everything's beauty. See, it's not just about planting, weeding, watering, and cleaning up the garden, though those practices are a part of the whole. It's about what makes something beautiful. It's you, quietly being you, the artist in the garden!

Chapter 8

Been There, Done That: Portraits of Outstanding Gardeners

I've been very fortunate during my years of growing and designing with plants to have known so many good people. In every aspect of life, these folks are determined to pursue a better thought and give it a try, and of course this extends to appreciating the rhythm, harmony, and sweet language of nature's design. Their work begins with the beauty of a plant, clean water, clean air, and healthy soil, but it also recognizes the various needs of human beings. Add understanding, purpose, perspective, and love, and you get something truly beautiful.

I want you to meet these exceptional folks and take a look at what they're doing. You may find that what they've accomplished inspires. You'll also find an aspirational reflection of your own efforts to enliven the place you live, to share its beauty with others—while having fun, of course.

Jeff Epping

Jeff is the director of horticulture at Olbrich Botanical Gardens in Madison, Wisconsin. His own nature mirrors the gardens he creates—it reflects their health and beauty and the essence of their style and relationships. Thought by thought, piece by piece, Jeff develops graceful meadows.

Inspired by meadows in England, Jeff sought out experienced turf people to develop a blend of fine fescues with an endurance and spirit unlike conventional bluegrass/perennial rye turf, and sowed the resulting mix in a few undeveloped areas at the botanic garden. The following fall, he and his crew planted 15,000 minor bulbs among the grasses; and for several falls thereafter, they added another 2,000 to 3,000 bulbs to the planting. Today the gardens thrive without fertilizer, require only two mowings a year, and need irrigation only in extreme heat or drought. The meadows bloom a full six to eight weeks in spring.

Following upon this success, Jeff has developed large meadows of *Carex pensylvanica* and *C. eburnea* and has also underplanted many of his shrub borders with other sedges. In a different vein, in the last few years he has embraced the gravel garden concept enhanced and promoted by Cassian Schmidt, whose profile follows.

If these ideas appeal, you could plant something similar. Just go slightly beyond what's easy; go beyond sameness. Jeff's love for what he does drove him to look for answers to everyday questions in different directions, and fortunately for us he has been generous in sharing his solutions.

A bulb-studded fescue meadow at Olbrich Botanical Gardens.

Cassian Schmidt

Cassian Schmidt is horticultural director at Hermann-shof, a fantastic Sichtungsgarten ("viewing garden") in the small town of Weinheim, Germany. When I walked through Cassian's gardens there, I saw beautiful plantings that included many of our Midwest natives. It was almost too nice. Cassian asked if I had looked at the soil. I hadn't. So I pushed the plants aside and saw that the soil was covered in ¼-inch to ⅜-inch stone chips. Immediately I thought of the way that gravel mulch is used in America—lightly covering the soil and used mainly for effect. Weeds push through; when you dig and divide plants, the soil gets in the gravel; more weeds sprout, and constant weeding becomes the norm. Or even worse, the ground is covered with weed mat, slits are cut about 2 feet apart, planted, then the mat is covered in gravel. This is bad for so many reasons. Then I remembered I was in a great garden in Germany, and something had to be different. So I asked Cassian to tell me why he was using gravel. Here's a summary of his approach.

His regional soils, like ours, are filled with weed seeds that have only one ambition: to germinate readily, grow quickly, and produce seed heavily. The challenge, Cassian decided, was to thwart that ambition. He decided to cover the soil with 4½ to 5 inches of clean granite chips. The granite chips would not support the cultural needs of the weeds, and the thickness of the chip layer would prevent their seeds from germinating.

The next part of the plan was to select plants that thrive in lean, well-drained soil. Where did he seek them out? In Missouri. He knew that many of our Midwest natives thrive in those conditions, and he found that plants grown in 4- to 4½-inch containers established most quickly. Because he needed the plants to fill in densely, he placed them 10 to 12 inches apart. His planting method: push the gravel aside until you barely see the soil below; take the plant out of the pot and place it in; then backfill with the gravel. You're finished! By mid-June you shouldn't be able to see the gravel.

He watered frequently at first, since gravel does not hold moisture. In similar situations you might need to water every three days. After four to six weeks, most of the plants had rooted into the soil below the gravel. The test for this is to tug lightly on the plant. At this point, watering could be reduced to maybe once every 10 days. The second season Cassian was done watering; rainfall was all that was necessary. In Cassian's system, the gravel and crown of the plants coexist happily. Water rushes quickly by the crown of the plant, unlike the conditions you find with organic/clay soils that retain more moisture for longer periods of time. The drier crown corresponds to the conditions the plants have evolved in. The plants are healthy.

Weeding is minimal. Most early weeds come from the soil within the containers of the plants. But weeds have difficulty germinating and living in dry gravel, and the maturing plants will also easily outcompete the few seedlings that develop.

In late fall or early spring the garden needs to be cut back and cleaned thoroughly, all debris removed. You want to leave very little plant litter: what remains from year to year can start creating an organic layer in the gravel, and thus weed seeds would have an easier time germinating and finding moisture to promote strong growth. The plants' nutritional needs are met by the organic matter in the soil below the gravel and the constant addition of organic matter through the living and dying of the roots of the plants in the garden. Cool!

But there's one major consideration with this style of gardening: you can't move plants and add new elements as you do in a traditional perennial garden. Once you disturb the soil and it gets mixed into the gravel, the weeds will spring up. Keep in mind, that's what weeds do—they patiently wait for opportunities.

Once I heard Cassian's description of the process, I couldn't wait to get home and develop a garden like the one I'd just seen. In June 2008 I planted our gravel garden around Northwind's freestanding boulder pyramid. As I write this in early 2013, I have yet to weed or water! We cut back all the plants and clean the gravel well in November.

This kind of gravel garden can provide endless options for turf areas, parking lots, or any open space that needs a better look. It would also appeal to someone who wants a garden with very little to do: there are plenty of busy people with other passions who still want to enjoy the beauty of plants.

Cassian Schmidt's gravel gardens have given us a system of planting that's smart, good-looking, and very economical. Such beauty can be the central theme in all our city parking lots and street medians—any place labor needs to be reduced, mowing cut, and mulch eliminated.

Marji Hess

We awaken each morning trusting the future with our dreams. Marji Hess, garden manager at the Gary Comer Youth Center in Chicago, deeply values the role our kids will play in enhancing their communities in that future. Using classroom time indoors and out, Marji and her colleagues combine purpose, compassion, ingenuity, teamwork, and fun to introduce teens to the dynamic world of nature, teaching them how to grow and care for plants, and how to share that newfound knowledge with their neighbors. The "classrooms" consist of an 8,100-square-foot rooftop garden and a 1¾-acre youth education garden built on a reclaimed brown site; together the sites produced 5,500 pounds of produce in 2012. "I just love the 'ah-ha' moment a young person has when they taste a strawberry, or dig in the soil, or get wowed by some aspect of nature," says Marji. "The outside world is teeming with opportunities to foster curiosity—the first step in anything, right? First someone has to ask a question. And then we take it from there."

With Marji's coaching, students are not only learning, they're doing, helping to maintain the plantings around the youth center, and teaching, giving demonstrations at the nearby farmers' market. To help promote urban beauty, I am working with her and youth center staff to create an onsite perennial nursery that will supply local landscape contractors; my hope is that this program will teach teens job skills, providing them with a possible career path. The impact Marji and everyone at the center has on kids and on the entire South Side community is profound. Marji says, "I learned from people who were truly passionate about the outside world, and that's a passion that has carried me through my whole life. Now I'm getting to be that person in someone else's life."

Most folks realize the value of sharing our knowledge and skills with others. If we stop asking questions, stop learning, stop creating solutions, that detached behavior encourages indifference, boredom, and spending too much time watching Fox News. The Gary Comer Youth Center's activity inspires today and enlivens tomorrow. We should all do the same: be both a teacher and a good student!

Lessons at the Gary Comer Youth Center can begin as students walk by the rooftop garden, with its tonal changes of green and random drifts of *Geranium sanguineum* 'Max Frei'.

Jennifer Davit

Jennifer took over as director and head horticulturist for Chicago's Lurie Garden in March 2010, following in the footsteps of Colleen Lockovitch, who nurtured Piet Oudolf's plant design vision in the young garden so well. Jennifer began by spending valuable time in the garden, watching the interactions between the plant communities and the tens of thousands of people who visit the garden each year, and then she talked to Piet to confirm and deepen her understanding of his intent, a style developed in harmony with place. Her goal? To maintain the health and artistry of that style and to share Piet's notion of dynamic beauty with all visitors.

How do most of us learn and develop our gardening methods and beliefs? Through example. Jennifer realizes that in many parks and gardens the visiting experience is "the experience," and she has found ways—through programs, garden walks, and garden practices—to deepen each visitor's understanding of a larger plant community, a sustainable ecosystem in the heart of one of the country's largest cities. I have discovered from Jennifer's style of presentation the significance of getting people involved by getting them excited about the plantings, the process, and the place. I have learned from her the true value of interpretation. Wouldn't anyone value and enjoy a place that talks to you, telling you why it's here and how it lives?

Jennifer implements a natural systems approach to caring for the planting—no chemicals or manufactured fertilizers. In early March, conditions permitting, the entire garden is cut back with mulching mowers. Nothing is removed, nothing brought in. Plants not only live, they positively thrive in their own litter. Sound familiar? People like Jennifer are necessary, not to keep introducing the next new plant or garden product, but to show by example how each of us can raise the level of beauty by the level of our intelligent care. Thank you, Jennifer.

At Chicago's Lurie Garden, Jennifer Davit makes sure the garden is a learning experience for even the youngest visitors.

Tom Wolfe

Both at home and at the Art Institute of Chicago, where he is head gardener, Tom Wolfe lives surrounded by nature—planting, nurturing, and immersing himself in the beauty of plants. He believes his garden in the heart of Chicago is an oasis, a place apart: "It separates us from work. It's a respite—even if it's just for lunch."

Tom started at the Art Institute 32 years ago. There were no boulevard plantings, Grant Park was open fields, and the Art Institute's neighbor was a train yard, not Millennium Park. At that time the grounds were a low priority—no one expected Tom to do more than to just keep things neat, tidy, and inviting to the public. But Tom took it beyond that, pruning long-neglected trees and shrubs, introducing new, characterful woody plantings, and establishing an integrated pest management program. In 1982, he had 73 large urns designed and made especially for the front of the building on Michigan Avenue. The response was wonderful! Their colorful seasonal display was a major spur to Mayor Daley's beautification program. Recently, he noticed decline in some towering 60-foot locusts that had been started from seed for the Art Institute in 1940. The trees had been growing in large, aboveground planters for decades, but their roots were no longer taking up water and nutrients. Tom went to heroic lengths to prune and reinvigorate the roots, and the trees responded beautifully.

I've had the opportunity to design and plant a few gardens with Tom at the Art Institute. Each time he updates the landscape, he incorporates more sustainable plants that he hopes will get his visitors thinking about landscapes in a new way. As budgets get reduced, he handily demonstrates how gardening knowledge and principles relate at once to inspiring landscapes and managed costs. For many years, Tom's passion has awakened passersby to the giving beauty of nature. The next time you walk outside, stop and look around. Is your garden doing the same?

Tom Wolfe's early work included pruning 36 ignored cockspur hawthorns in the Art Institute of Chicago's South Garden, designed by noted modernist Dan Kiley. The layered, horizontal branching effect reflects the essence of the building.

Christine Nye

The Shedd Aquarium is the most visited site in Chicago. But take a walk around the building before you enter. You'll see sand gardens, wetlands, waterfalls, rock out-croppings, vegetable and perennial gardens, mixed borders for bird habitat, beehives, fescue meadows, prairie-inspired plantings, rain gardens, and turf. Somewhere within all these polycultural habitats you will find Christine, the horticultural manager there. She wants you to know that nature isn't something that exists somewhere "out there"—it's right beneath your feet. For 20 years she's spent every working day patiently restoring the local ecosystem and showing schoolchildren and other visitors how they can do the same. Revitalizing compacted, urban soil is important to her; at the aquarium, she's fortified it with organic matter and compost tea. She never uses chemicals on her plants; she grows a lot of vegetables on the site, and she doesn't want to harm pollinators and other wildlife—including people—who enjoy her edibles.

One of her goals is to get folks "to appreciate the beauty of their food." Another is to develop diverse, nature-friendly plantings. "We're building back the ecosystem," she says. "There are so many birds and insects around the building, it's miraculous." Christine is deeply committed to the urgent practice of managing our remnant prairies, understanding how much we can learn from them. But as much as she loves them, she recognizes that not everyone can embrace prairies in urban and suburban landscapes. She likes the new nature-inspired garden styles that use a variety of plants to emulate the prairie. "It's a way to give people the nature of prairie but in a language they can understand," she says. "It's given us this other set of paints in our box." Christine hopes to educate people about the decisions they make that affect the environment. She says, "I hope when people come they're inspired to do some gardening of their own and that they'll take home some of the principles I am showing them."

The landscapes around the Shedd are a blend of constant creativity, spirited imagination, concern and care for others, an open mind, and persistent dedication. Christine invites the open space around the Shedd Aquarium to awaken and contribute to the lives of many living creatures. With each passing year she grows wiser, eager to see the next bird migration.

Can your yard be more interesting, healthier, more welcoming? You can choose the plants, determine the styles, understand the care, and live in the garden connected to your work, the plants, and the insects and birds. The wholeness you enjoy and that you share with others can't exactly be measured, but you will know for a certainty that your time has been well spent when you and they see the goodness of a healthy garden.

Social change happens in many ways—including clear, info-rich signage, pointing out the benefits of Christine Nye's plantings at the Shedd Aquarium.

Noel Kingsbury

If you ask a question about how we garden, this individualistic plantsman has either thought about it already or knows someone pursuing the answer. I first met Noel at Piet and Anja Oudolf's home in the Netherlands. Later we got together when he brought a tour group from England to the Chicago/Milwaukee area to see our prairies; I met the group and walked them through the Chiwaukee. During that visit, I really began to appreciate Noel's knowledge and practices, so now I'd like to share with you his thoughts, in his own words:

Gardening for me is about a conversation with nature. One of my biggest inspirations in gardening is natural or semi-natural plant communities: wildflower meadows, prairies, peat bogs, and woodlands. Much as I enjoy historic or formal gardens, it is these wild plant communities that really excite and inspire me. I'm fascinated about how they work, why particular plants grow in particular places, why certain species always seem to be found together, and especially how some plants survive in really hostile-looking environments.

I see gardening, this direct engagement with plants, very much as editing or managing natural processes, guiding the long-term development of living things, each with its own agenda. This in fact is what ecology is all about—what happens when plants or other living things relate and interact. When we look at a wild plant community, what we see is the end result of many years of a variety of processes—it is these processes that ecology tries to understand, to interpret, and even predict. In gardening I try to apply my understanding and make use of these processes—so that I can combine long-lived plants, short-lived ones, spreading ones, seeding ones, persistent ones, etc.

Gardeners, I believe, should not stay at home. They should get out and see what plants can do in the wild—and by wild, I do not mean just wilderness, but roadsides, waste ground, abandoned fields, anywhere managed by nature rather than man. They should get down on their hands and knees and get "the rabbit's-eye view," seeing what the plant does at ground level. Close observation of plants, as well as seeing how they perform en masse, will do much to teach us well as to inspire.

One more thing about Noel: he's easy for you to get to know, too, through his website, magazine articles, and books, including those he has co-authored with Piet Oudolf (see the recommended reading section).

Noel Kingsbury continues to pursue planting practices and spaces that traditionally have been marginalized, approached indifferently, or ignored. Thanks to him, this street intersection has "given way" to a higher level of beauty.

Terry Guen

In 2001 I was tapped to assist with the growing, sourcing, and installation of plants for Piet Oudolf's Lurie Garden in Millennium Park. Terry Guen was the lead landscape architect, and soon thereafter we began working together. After a few meetings, I began to see in her someone who cared deeply about how the planting would be carried out. Terry balances her knowledge with the overall project goals and reaches out to others who have different areas of expertise. Most landscape architects design and plant using traditional methods—their silver bullet. But Terry wanted to know what the "best practices" would be for Piet's plantings. She responded to them thoughtfully and enhanced them when necessary in response to the unique rooftop conditions of the Lurie Garden, making solid choices and following the flow of the process intimately to completion. She was determined to provide healthy conditions for plants, so that they would live well for many years. Such a good beginning is directly related to this or any project's success.

Terry is always thinking about how the landscape will meet the needs of the community. Her gift is the ability to turn even the toughest urban spaces—former parking lots, boulevards, airports, even reservoirs and pumping stations—into spaces where plants grow, wildlife returns, and people reconnect with each other and with nature. Her designs inspire and educate entire neighborhoods; and her interactive approach, involving the people that live where her projects are located, has influenced me greatly. When I think about Terry and her commitment to connect healthy plantings to all people, I see so much more of what I could be doing.

What about you? We all live in a community of people, sharing with them the streets, sidewalks, parks, schools, churches, stores, and comforts of life. What could be better than contributing to the overall health of your total community, strengthening your relationship with the folks who live nearby? Could your beautiful back yard inspire a beautiful neighborhood park? It's not just about you, or the plants: it's about us!

Terry Guen designs for city people, encouraging their participation in the urban neighborhood and supporting its strength with lively, well-thought-out plantings.

Piet Oudolf

Though I didn't meet Piet until the late summer of 2001, I felt I already knew this acclaimed plantsman and designer through a few of his books. The first, much more than a simple A-to-Z of ornamental grasses, discussed mixed plantings incorporating grasses and perennials that lived well together and created dynamic styles. Standard practice up to this time had been to plant perennials in large masses; but because the plants weren't dug up and divided every year or two, these large single-species plantings declined and needed to be replaced. Prairie restoration groups were planting mixed native plants but gave little consideration to style or composition; if the plants were native and living roughly in the proper habitat, everything was swell. So what did our landscapes become? Stock beds of declining perennials, and prairie re-creations that were ecologically sensible but that didn't involve thoughtful, artistic composition. You could visit any nature center and find big bluestem and prairie dock falling over the sidewalks. Seeing plantings like this, with no supporting grasses, did not inspire people to use native plants in their home landscapes.

Piet Oudolf has had a profound effect on this situation. His designs are plant-based and inspired by nature. He says, "Gardening, for me, becomes looking at and understanding plants, the communities they are from. You have to see the beauty in everything. The landscape is so alive, so poetic." Piet recreates the look of meadows, woodlands, rivers, and dunes, evoking, in the process, the feelings those places create in us. "I want my designs to look wild but with the plants behaving," he explains. Piet was schooled in traditional, formal gardens, but he soon became impatient with what he calls "the rules"—all the deadheading, staking, and maintenance that was required. For nearly 40 years now he has been studying how plants grow—not just throughout a season but over the years.

Piet's inspiration, guide, and great partner is his wife, Anja. For many years they worked together: while Piet designed gardens, Anja managed their nursery in Arnhem, the Netherlands. They traveled throughout Europe and the United States, looking for plants that were long-lived, tolerant of many soil conditions, well behaved, and resistant to insects and diseases—plants that performed well without deadheading or staking, provided interesting structure, and looked good in every phase of their lives. Together they have defined a new style of planting.

As Piet says, "I always look for the possibilities in plants." When he designed the Lurie Garden, he included plants seldom used in horticulture—*Eragrostis spectabilis*, *Ruellia humilis*, *Lythrum alatum*, *Echinacea pallida*—and used more regional native plants than any landscape architect or garden designer in the Chicago area had done previously. He valued their durability and structure, and the way they grow in communities. He also pushed the idea of diversity—which provided a crucial opportunity for many plants that had been patiently waiting to show their stuff.

His influence encourages us all to look beyond the flower color and bloom time of a plant, to look deeper into its generous nature and year-round character. We have all grown up looking at gorgeous flowers—it's hard not to. But each of us needs to learn the richer beauty of the whole plant. Piet's gardens show us why that effort is worth it.

The beauty of Piet Oudolf's plantings on New York's High Line draws people—now walking, not hurrying—into the moment, calming the day, engaging the senses. Our culture desperately needs this connection.

Epilogue

Gardening holds as many experiences as there are individuals to have them. For millenia, people have been writing about plants and gardens, why we garden, how we garden, the importance of gardens—myriad thoughts from folks in all walks of life. So what do you think? Whatever you think or feel, don't stop engaging—nurture these new feelings, bring them into the next moment. Keep reading garden columns and blogs, buying books, and visiting gardens—not just botanic gardens or arboretums, but the gardens of your neighbors and friends, the empty lot on the corner, or a nature preserve not far from your home. And whether you're caught up in the scale of the space or the details of an abundant sliver of a garden alongside a garage, look beyond the entertainment, the first attraction. What you find and learn will make you shake with excitement. You're connected.

It's all about community. I end this book thanking all the wonderful people I've learned so much from. And my hope is that when you dig for what each person finds important, when you witness how they approach their work—with belief, curiosity, imagination, passion, persistence, and love—you too will see what a huge difference that exploration can make in all our lives.

Happy gardening!

Recommended Reading

Berry, Wendell. 2011. *Leavings: Poems*. Berkeley, Calif.: Counterpoint.

Bryson, Charles T., and Michael S. DeFelice, eds. 2010. *Weeds of the Midwestern United States and Central Canada*. Athens: University of Georgia Press.

Cullina, William. 2009. *Understanding Perennials*. Boston: Houghton Mifflin Harcourt.

Darke, Rick. 2007. *The Encyclopedia of Grasses for Livable Landscapes*. Portland, Ore.: Timber Press.

DiSabato-Aust, Tracy. 2006. *The Well-Tended Perennial Garden*. Portland, Ore.: Timber Press.

Gardens Illustrated. Bristol, U.K.: Immediate Media Company.

Gingras, Pierre. 2001. *Bulbs for All Seasons*. Richmond Hill, Ont.: Firefly Books.

Grese, Robert E., ed. 2011. *The Native Landscape Reader*. Amherst: University of Massachusetts Press.

Hipp, Andrew L. 2008. *Sedges: An Introduction to the Genus* Carex *(Cyperaceae)*. Madison: University of Wisconsin Press.

Hustvedt, Siri. 2006. *Mysteries of the Rectangle: Essays on Painting*. New York: Princeton Architectural Press.

King, Michael, and Piet Oudolf. 1998. *Gardening with Grasses*. Portland, Ore.: Timber Press.

Kingsbury, Noel. 2006. *Seedheads in the Garden*. Portland, Ore.: Timber Press.

Lowenfels, Jeff, and Wayne Lewis. 2010. *Teaming with Microbes*. Rev. ed. Portland, Ore.: Timber Press.

Mabey, Richard. 2011. *Weeds: In Defense of Nature's Most Unloved Plants*. New York: Ecco.

Mickel, John. 2003. *Ferns for American Gardens*. Portland, Ore.: Timber Press.

Oliver, Mary. 2005. *New and Selected Poems, Volume One*. Rev. ed. Boston: Beacon Press.

Oudolf, Piet, and Noel Kingsbury. 1999. *Designing with Plants*. Portland, Ore.: Timber Press.

———. 2013. *Planting: A New Perspective*. Portland, Ore.: Timber Press.

Swink, Floyd, and Gerould Wilhelm. 2012. *Plants of the Chicago Region*. Bloomington: Indiana University Press.

Willsdon, Clare A. P. 2004. *In the Gardens of Impressionism*. New York: The Vendome Press.

Woelfle-Erskine, Cleo, and Apryl Uncapher. 2012. *Creating Rain Gardens*. Portland, Ore.: Timber Press.

Photo Credits

Pages 70 (right) and 71 (right) by Jill Selinger.

Pages 28, 71 (middle), 78 (right), 85 (right), and 119 (left) by Brent Heath.

Page 75 courtesy Wikimedia Commons / Karelj.

Page 76 (left) courtesy Wikimedia Commons / Michael Wolf.

Page 82 courtesy Wikimedia Commons / Chmee2.

Page 85 (left) courtesy University of Michigan Herbarium / Russ Schipper.

Pages 86, 99 (right), 100 (left), and 108 (top) courtesy Midwest Groundcovers.

Pages 88 (left), 102 (right), 111 (right), and 119 (right) courtesy Northcreek Nursery.

Page 102 (left) courtesy Wikimedia Commons / Walter Siegmund.

Pages 18, 103, 108 (bottom), 196, and 206 by Piet Oudolf.

Page 105 (left) courtesy Wikimedia Commons / Meneerke bloem.

Page 116 (left) courtesy Missouri Botanical Garden Plant-Finder / Tammy Palmier.

Page 118 (right) courtesy Flikr / Erutuon.

Page 192 by Brent Horvath.

Pages 120 and 198 by Jeff Epping.

Page 201 by Jennifer Davit.

Page 203 © Linda Oyama Bryan.

Page 204 by Noel Kingsbury.

Page 205 by Terry Guens.

All other photographs are by the author.

Index